ANGELA,

*"You don't lose yourself
when you follow the leader.
Rather, you can become better
than you ever were before."*

Ruben Gonzalez

To book Ruben to speak for your next
corporate meeting or event, call
832-689-8282

For more information, visit
TheLugeMan.com

The Shortcut

ISBN: 979-8-9865188-0-0

Olympia Press
832-689-8282

Praise for *The Shortcut*

"You'll want to share *The Shortcut* with your friends, family and co-workers. This instant classic is truly a gift for anyone who wants to succeed in life."

Jack Canfield, author of *The Success Principles*™

"Captivating from start to finish, you don't read this book, you live it. Anyone who's in sales needs to read *The Shortcut* immediately. You'll find yourself immersed in not just the story, but in the application."

Mark Hunter, "The Sales Hunter," author of *A Mind for Sales*

"Magnificent story filled with wisdom. If you lead a company, be sure everyone on your team has a copy to read and study. If you're a parent be sure your children do the same."

Bob Burg, coauthor of *The Go-Giver* and *Go-Giver Series*

"*The Shortcut* is filled with dozens of life-changing insights. Don't buy just one copy of this book – buy it for your children, your friends, and your co-workers. Thank you Ruben, for showing us how to make our dreams a reality!"

Mark Miller, VP of Leadership, Chick-fil-A, author of *The Heart of Leadership*

"This powerful story is packed with insights that will help you create a better future. Everyone from CEOs to high school students will gain from reading this gem."

Steven Pressfield, author of *The War of Art* and *Gates of Fire*

"A riveting story that at times brought a tear to my eye and at others a smile. I'll be handing out copies to the Wounded Warriors I coach. *The Shortcut* will surely improve their lives."

David Kimes, Olympian, 2X Shooting World Champion, Navy Wounded Warriors Shooting Coach

"A captivating business parable about accomplishing goals. Read *The Shortcut* and let Ruben's story inspire you to become the leader you want to be!"

Ken Blanchard, coauthor of *The New One Minute Manager* and *Leading at a Higher Level*

"*The Shortcut* is an engaging story filled with timeless principles that will help you reach your full potential."

Dave Ramsey, Bestselling Author and Radio Host

"Olympic champions are ordinary people who found a way to accomplish extraordinary things. If you want to learn how Olympians think and act, take *The Shortcut* and enjoy the wisdom and advice of mentors who have travelled that road. It worked for Ruben and it can work for you!"

John Naber, Olympic Champion, Author, Speaker, Broadcaster, Businessman

"Great read! Ruben delivers a wealth of insightful nuggets to help everyone achieve their goals in life. The approach he describes is a compelling vision of leadership and high performance. Highly recommended reading for anyone who wants to be a high achiever!"

Mickey Addison, Colonel, US Air Force, author of *The Five Be's: A Straightforward Guide to Life*

"I tell all of my fighters, invest in your dream and read this book. *The Shortcut* is a powerful parable that will not only inspire you to action but also gives practical steps for achieving at the highest levels. This book is a must read."

Bruce Babashan - USA Boxing & Pro Boxing Trainer, Speaker

"Follow the leader and you will learn the shortcut to success as others have done by following Ruben Gonzalez"

Don Green, Executive Director, The Napoleon Hill Foundation

"If you will read Ruben's books or listen to Ruben speak, your life will change for the positive."

Lou Holtz, Legendary Notre Dame Football Coach

"*The Shortcut* will keep you turning pages and learning critical business principles along the way! This fascinating story is poignant and relevant to the challenges so many leaders face in their lives and careers today. You won't want to put it down!"

Dr. Marshall Goldsmith, author of *The Earned Life, Triggers,* and *What Got You Here Won't Get You There*

"You won't be able to put down *The Shortcut*. It will speak to your heart, enlighten your thinking and inspire you to be the best you can be. You'll want to get a copy for your family, friends and co-workers."

Dr. Ivan Misner, Founder of BNI
NY Times Bestselling Author

"The path to reaching your goal is best learned by those who preceded you....so find your leader and never look back."

Rocky Bleier - 4X Super Bowl Champion, Vietnam Veteran

Foreword by Jack Canfield
author of *The Success Principles*™

The Shortcut

The Fastest Way
to Achieve Your Goals

by Four-time Olympian
Ruben Gonzalez

Olympia
Press

Why You Should Read this Book

by Jack Canfield, author of *The Success Principles*™

Once in a while, you discover a book that's so inspiring, that you find yourself making a list of people who *must* have a copy.

That's what happened to me after reading *The Shortcut*, by Olympian Ruben Gonzalez. I believe that after you read this book, you'll want to share it with your friends, family and co-workers. This instant classic is truly a gift for anyone who wants to succeed in life.

If I were to write out a list of people who would benefit from *The Shortcut*, here's who I'd include:

- **Employees and business associates** – for they'll learn how to achieve their goals faster.

- **Friends in management positions** – for they'll learn how to inspire their organizations to excel.

- **Family members** – for they'll discover how to reach their full potential so they can create a better future.

- **High school & college students** – for they'll learn success principles that will help them achieve lifelong success. Insights that are not taught in schools.

- **Athletes** – for they'll learn how to improve their game faster than they ever have before.

- Finally, anyone who has a goal or dream they are hungry to achieve.

Great fiction doesn't just entertain – it also educates. That's the case with *The Shortcut*. Ruben Gonzalez is the real deal. He practices what he teaches. When I heard about his incredible Olympic story – how he decided to take up the sport of luge at the age of 21 and how he went on to compete in four Winter Olympics in four different decades, I included his story in three chapters of my book *The Success Principles*™ – Believe in Yourself, Take Action, and Start Now.

Ruben has wrapped up truth and wisdom in a captivating story that will engage you and inspire you to fight for your goals and dreams. If you take Ruben's advice to heart, you'll start achieving your goals faster than you ever thought possible, and you'll become a better leader.

Read it, apply its wisdom, and share it.

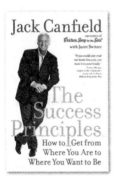

Jack Canfield
Author of *The Success Principles*™
Founder and Chairman of
The Canfield Training Group

How this Book Came to Be

After 20 years of speaking professionally all over the world, I did my first TED talk, *The Power of Following the Leader*. In it, I shared how I always resisted following my coaches' advice and how I paid the price – in luge injuries. After being a hardhead for three Olympics, I finally decided to trust my coach, let go, and follow the leader. As soon as I did, I started improving faster than I ever had in my whole career. Incredibly, I was sliding better at the age of 55 than I had ever before.

The TED talk struck a chord with a lot of people. After receiving positive comments, emails and letters from corporate leaders, life coaches, athletic coaches, pastors, teachers, principals and parents, all telling me how they were impacted by the talk, I decided to write this book.

The Shortcut is a parable about a young executive who needs to grow up and start following the leader, and how by following the leader he's able to achieve his goals faster and in turn he is able to become a better leader.

I hope *The Shortcut* helps you achieve your goals faster as well.

Ruben Gonzalez
Olympian, Author, Speaker
Colorado Springs, CO

Watch the TED talk that started it all, here:
FollowTheLeaderTEDtalk.com

Unhappy Valentine

Linda Shepherd, vice president of sales at prominent software company Garcia Munos IT Services, was meeting with Pablo Garcia Munos, its founder and CEO, to discuss their quarterly earnings.

Pablo smiled, closed his laptop, and rose from his desk as Linda walked into his office. "Good morning, Linda. How's your day going?"

"Busy, busy, but you know that's how I like it."

"Yes, I know – we both get bored easily, don't we?" he smiled. "So, tell me – how are the numbers looking this quarter?"

"Unfortunately, same as usual," said Linda. "One region is doing great, three are doing well, and one is dragging."

"Valentine?"

"Yes," she let out a heavy sigh. "Johnny Valentine's region has been underperforming the last three quarters. If we can just get him up to speed, the company's profits will go through the roof."

"What do you think's the problem?"

She rubbed her chin and looked down, "I honestly don't know. Johnny looks great on paper."

He had graduated from Wharton with honors with a double MBA in Marketing and Entrepreneurship; he was energetic, put in the hours, and was very confident. Linda paused to think for a second; maybe he was too confident. She pursed her lips. "He comes across as arrogant sometimes. He likes doing things his own way to the point that he resists taking direction from me." She stiffened. "He's 27 years old, but he really needs to grow up."

Pablo rested his chin on his hand. "Linda, would you call Valentine up so he can join us?"

Linda texted Johnny Valentine, and a few minutes later, Mary, Pablo's executive assistant, led him into Pablo's office. Pablo stood, flashed his disarming smile, and walked to the door. Linda followed.

Stretching out his hand, Pablo said, "Good morning, Johnny. Thanks for taking a few minutes of your valuable time to come up. I know that you're really busy with your team."

Johnny tried to stay cool even though he didn't know why he'd been called. "My pleasure, Pablo." After he and Linda exchanged pleasantries, Pablo opened his hand in a gesture for him to sit. They headed over to a corner of the office, where a leather sofa and two plush chairs lay.

"Johnny," Pablo began, "Tell me, how are things going in your region?"

Johnny pressed his lips together. "It's been a little slow, but we'll get over this."

"It's critical for our company that we increase your region's productivity. What can we do to help you out? How can we serve you?"

If I accept their help, I'll just look weak, Johnny thought. *It will make it look like I can't do my own job.* He knew the region had been struggling – not all his fault, surely – and that this conversation was a long-time coming, but Johnny wasn't about to admit that he was failing.

"Thank you, Pablo, but I'm okay. I have it under control."

Pablo stiffened, and his eyes met Linda's for an instant.

"Control?" Pablo wrote the word control on his pad.

"Hmm." Linda's voice deepened. "You know, control is an illusion... You don't need to be in control to be successful."

2

Johnny's eyes narrowed. He looked confused. Were Pablo and Linda trying to trap him?

Pablo walked over to his desk, looked at some spreadsheets, lowered his voice, and said, "Johnny, your region's been underperforming for the last three quarters. I'm sorry, but unless you can turn things around by the end of this quarter, we're going to have to let you go."

Linda's jaw dropped. What was Pablo doing?

"You don't have to do this by yourself, Johnny. Linda and I are willing to help you out." Then, suddenly, Pablo looked at his watch and said, "That's all."

Johnny left Pablo's office; his abruptness left him in a daze. Suddenly, he started sweating from the shock. He'd never been in a position like this before.

Back in Pablo's office, Linda looked at her boss and shook her head in disbelief. "Pablo, I sure wasn't expecting you to do that. Wasn't that a bit harsh? It's not like you."

"I know it seems abrupt, but when Johnny said he had the situation under control, everything suddenly made sense."

"What do you mean?"

Pablo held his palms up. "You told me that Johnny resists your direction and wants to do everything his own way. His need for control is keeping him from following you. I needed to shock him so that he'll hopefully see that he can go further by following the leader than he can ever go on his own."

"I see," Linda nodded, though she was still a little confused.

"Have you ever heard the saying, 'When the student is ready, the teacher will appear?'"

Linda nodded, "Sure, many times."

3

"Well, I need to find out really quickly if our student is ready. Hopefully, he'll ask for help. Just in case, start looking for someone who can run Johnny's region."

You Have to Grow

Johnny was shocked. For the rest of the day, he could barely focus on his work. The only thing he could think about was that if he lost his job, his life would change overnight. He rubbed his fingers over his temples. He tried to think of a way to increase his region's productivity, but he was too emotionally overwhelmed. How could this happen to him? He slammed his fist on his desk. He was a top-ranked MBA graduate, and he worked harder than anyone he knew.

Johnny looked up at a framed picture from his high school baseball days. He had been blessed with great athletic ability. He was fast, powerful, agile, and quick-thinking. He had lettered in three sports in high school, and he'd expected to get a baseball college scholarship, but the offers never came. He never knew why. He looked down and slowly shook his head.

Several colleges had been interested in Johnny, but after talking with his high school coaches and finding out how he was uncoachable, that he resisted following his coach's advice, their interest had quickly disappeared.

By 4:45 PM, Johnny couldn't stand it anymore: he called Mary and asked if there was any way he could speak with Pablo.

A few minutes later, Mary called him back. "Mr. Valentine, Mr. Munos has a few minutes right now if you'd still like to come up."

He slowly exhaled and closed his eyes. "I'll be there right away. Thank you, Mary."

Mary escorted Johnny into Pablo's office. Pablo had a big smile on his face.

"Johnny, I'm so glad you decided to come back up. How can I serve you?"

"Thanks for seeing me, Pablo." Pablo smiled. "I've been trying to process what you said to me earlier, but I'm so shocked that I can barely think." Johnny felt a tightness in his chest and shook his head in frustration. "Ever since I've been here, I've worked as hard as possible, but I haven't been able to make any headway with my region. I've tried everything. Maybe I'm just not cut out to be a regional manager."

Pablo sighed. The truth was, Johnny was a good employee: reliable and a hard worker. He just needed a push.

"We hired you because we believe you have what it takes. You're just not using all of it yet. I'm not talking about working harder – you work hard enough. I'm talking about something else."

Pablo walked over to his coffee bar. "Care for a cup of coffee?

"Just some water, please."

Pablo made himself an espresso and brought Johnny a glass of water.

"What do you think I need to do to turn my region around?"

"It's not about doing; it's about *being*. Who do you have to *be* to turn your region around? That's the question you need to ask yourself, Johnny."

Johnny furrowed his brow. "I don't understand."

"You can improve your life because you have the ability to change. In life, you don't get what you want – you get what you are. If you want more, you need to grow. Only then will you be able to get better results."

Johnny leaned forward and took a deep breath but didn't reply. Pablo took it as confirmation to continue. "Your best thinking got you to this point. If you want to go higher, you need higher thinking. You need bigger, better ideas."

Intrigued, Johnny looked up. "What kind of ideas?"

"Well, I can't just tell you – that wouldn't help you. You need to discover them on your own."

Johnny dropped his head in his hands. He slowly shook his head back and forth in a gesture of exasperation. Would this be the end of his job?

"Here's what I want you to do... Go home, relax, and get a good night's sleep. Think about anything but work. If anything, think about the best coaches, teachers, or leaders you've ever had – the people who made the biggest impact in your life. Think about what made them so special.

"Tomorrow morning, before work, I want you to go to Cafe Olympia. If you're truly ready, you'll find your answers there."

Johnny squinted and tilted his head, utterly confused, as Pablo continued, "Johnny, I believe in you."

He stood and guided Johnny out the door before they parted with one last bit of advice from the CEO: "Rest up, and remember – Cafe Olympia."

Cafe Olympia

Johnny was more confused than ever. How would a coffee shop help him turn his region around?

When he got home, he plopped down on his couch and turned on a baseball game. But he just stared into space. Within a few minutes, he was sound asleep.

The TV was still on when he woke up the next morning. He'd slept all night on the couch. Johnny looked up at the clock and couldn't believe it – 9:28 AM! He smacked his hand on his forehead. He was already almost two hours late for work – just what he needed with his job on the line. He ran through the shower, got dressed, and sped out the door.

As soon as he pulled into the Garcia Munos IT Services parking lot, he saw Pablo's car and remembered – Cafe Olympia!

He pounded his fist on the steering wheel, "I don't even know where Cafe Olympia's at!"

He quickly looked it up and found the address: 1964 Innsbruck St., right in the middle of the museum district.

The outside of Cafe Olympia looked like an old European restaurant: ornate windows with a beautiful sign that read, "Cafe Olympia, Coffee and Wisdom Served Here."

As soon as he walked inside, his jaw dropped, and the tension left his body. He felt like he'd been transported back in time. This was by far the most beautiful coffee shop he'd ever been in. The wood paneling, the lighting, the floors, the tables and chairs, the decorations – everything looked like an old café you might see in Rome, Paris, or Vienna.

The place was packed. Every table was taken – in the middle of the morning! He narrowed his eyes. Something didn't seem right. Then he realized what it was: not a single person was working on a laptop. Everyone was talking – couples, professionals, and people old enough to be retired. The buzz was amazing.

A waiter and a waitress were serving the tables like at a restaurant. It looked like they could have used a couple of more waiters – that's how busy the café was.

As Johnny reached the counter, he remembered how late for work he was.

Carl, a middle-aged-looking barista, smiled and asked him, "What will it be?"

"I'll have a large caramel Frappuccino to go," Johnny said in a sharp tone, not even looking at the barista.

Dmitry Feld, an older-aged Ukrainian regular who was standing at the bar nursing an espresso, chuckled.

"Sorry, partner," said Carl, "this is a traditional European café – we don't serve Frappuccinos, and we don't make coffee to-go. We only serve traditional coffee drinks and only in ceramic espresso and coffee cups." He pointed to the menu behind him that had "Espresso," "Cappuccino," and "Latte" scrawled in pastel-blue chalk.

Frustrated and flustered, Johnny wheeled about on the spot and went to make a mad dash for the doorway when Dmitry called back, "Listen, hotshot!"

Johnny whirled around and was about to object to being called "hotshot," but when he looked at Dmitry, his warm smile, his Santa-like twinkling eyes, and his charismatic way drew him in, disarming him.

"Life's too short to be rushing all the time," Dmitry smiled. "It's not good for the soul." He paused, "Breathe…. slow down…. enjoy life." He gently spread his arms. "Why don't you try the double espresso? You can thank me later."

Johnny checked the time, looked at Carl, and muttered, "Double espresso. In a ceramic cup."

"You got it, boss. It will be a few minutes." Carl pointed to the tables and firmly said, "I'm making drinks for them too. You're number 12 in line. Dmitry, why don't you show him around?"

Dmitry thrust a large hand out in front of Johnny "What's your name? I'm Dmitry."

"Valentine, Johnny Valentine." He gave him a hard handshake. "Where are you from? I can't tell if your accent is East Texas or London, England."

"Kyiv, Ukraine. Came to the U.S. when I was 24. I LOVE America! Best country in the world." He grinned widely, "In America, as long as you're willing to work hard, you can make your dream come true."

Johnny bared his teeth. "I work hard, and I might be losing my job soon," he said bitterly.

Dmitry looked directly at the young man's eyes and pointed at him, "Maybe it's not *your* dream."

Johnny paused, thinking, but then quickly changed the subject. "So, what's the deal with this place? I've never been to a coffee shop that looked like this."

"We wanted to do something special. Something unique." He thrust his chest out. "Something different, that made a difference in people's lives. We decided it would be a special coffee shop."

Johnny's eyes opened wide. "Wait a minute. You own Cafe Olympia?"

"I'm one of the partners. We're best friends and partners."

"I see."

Dmitry started gesturing with his arms. "We spent a summer in Italy and looked at hundreds of them. We

11

worked our way from Sicily all the way to Piedmont, up in the Alps, from the Mediterranean to the Austrian border.

"At first, our idea was to take the best things from all the coffee shops we saw, then incorporate them into a coffee shop here in America. But you know the old saying, 'When man makes a plan, God laughs.'"

Johnny nodded; oh, he knew all too well about man's "best-laid plans."

Dmitry shrugged and lifted his hands. "God had a different plan for us." He explained that when they got to Cortina d'Ampezzo – a beautiful village at the foot of the Dolomites – they saw the perfect café right next to the old bobsled track, the Cafe Olympia. Cortina hosted the 1956 Winter Olympics, and they had a rich Winter Olympic heritage.

"Cafe Olympia had been run by the same family for almost a hundred years," Dmitry continued. "It had all the things we liked best from all the Italian cafés we had visited and then some." His eyes sparkled. "And it was for sale! The whole thing was a miracle.

"Fortunately, we saw the light. We saw the opportunity. We bought Cafe Olympia, had it carefully dismantled, and rebuilt it here. We didn't change a thing – even the black and white floor tiles are from the original café."

Johnny rubbed his chin. "What do you mean, *fortunately* you saw the light?"

Dmitry said, "Have you ever heard the expression, 'Pride cometh before the fall?'" Johnny nodded. "Do you know where that expression is from?" He had to admit that he didn't.

"It's from the book of Proverbs in the Bible," he said firmly. "King Solomon was the richest and wisest man in Israel. He wrote the book of Proverbs to share his wisdom.

Proverbs 16:18 says, 'Pride goes before destruction, and haughtiness before a fall.'"

Dmitry continued, "Many times, people let their pride get in the way of achieving their goals. They want to control every step of the way instead of being open to new ideas. Fortunately, we were open to creating our special café in a completely different way than we originally thought we would."

Johnny cocked his head in disbelief. "But didn't it cost you much more to dismantle, ship, and rebuild the café?" he asked. "Wouldn't it have been smarter to shoot some pictures of it and build a similar one?"

"We wanted it to be special. Unique. One-of-a-kind. And along the way, we came to understand that we didn't want it to be a copy; we wanted it to be authentic. Real. Filled with character and history. We wanted it to touch people's hearts and souls."

Dmitry and Johnny turned their heads and slowly looked around the café.

"Tell me something: what did you feel when you first walked into Cafe Olympia?"

Johnny closed his eyes and smiled with his whole face, "Hmm… I felt like I'd gone back in time and that I had been transported to another place. It felt like what traveling in a time machine must feel like."

"You haven't even tasted the coffee yet. Would you want to come back?"

"Absolutely. And I'd want to share Cafe Olympia with my friends. Judging from the incredible scent, the coffee can't be too bad."

"We only buy the finest beans," he said with a gleam in his eye. "And we roast them right here."

"Valentine, double espresso!" announced Carl.

Johnny tasted the coffee; it was ambrosia, nectar of the gods. His whole body went slack. "Oh my gosh. This is incredible. Now I see why you don't need to sell Frappuccinos."

Johnny tipped his head back to sip more of the delicious liquid. He pointed up and smirked. "What's up with all the toy sleds hanging from the ceiling? Do you all sell toys too?" he chuckled.

Carl and Dmitry looked at each other and slowly shook their heads exasperatedly.

Dmitry pointed to a picture on the wall. "See that picture? The one with the map of India on it? Would you read what it says?"

Johnny looked at a framed picture; it had a saying. The walls of Cafe Olympia were filled with similar framed quotes.

"'To conceal ignorance is to increase it,'" he parroted.

"You know who said that?"

Johnny jutted his chin and puffed his chest out – more questions that left him feeling a lot dumber than he considered himself to be. "No, who?"

"Gandhi, a pretty smart man. Now, look at that picture over there. What does it say?"

Johnny sighed. "'You're either green and growing or ripe and rotting.'"

"Do you know what that means?"

Johnny raised an eyebrow and smiled. "Some kind of agricultural wisdom from the Midwest?"

Dmitry stiffened – obviously that wasn't the right thing for Johnny to say. "It means that as soon as you think you've arrived, as soon as you're ripe, you're about to go down in flames. Pride goes before the fall. You always want to be green and growing. Always wanting to learn

14

more, to take your craft to a higher level. Arrogant people are ripe and rotting. Humble people are green and growing."

Johnny cleared his throat. Was Dmitry making fun of him? Johnny had a big ego. He knew that he was a good-looking, intelligent guy. He also knew that he could be arrogant at times. More than once, someone had told Johnny that he was a know-it-all filled with false confidence.

"You know what we call people like you where I come from?" Dmitry asked.

"No, what?" He raised his chin and leaned forward.

"We call them confidently ignorant – they sound like they know, but they don't know." He sighed, "Be real. Be genuine. People will like you more if you're real – and you have to be real before people will trust you."

Johnny paused for a few seconds, pursed his lips and said, "I guess." Then he looked back up and asked, "So, what's so special about the sleds?"

Dmitry stood tall. "Those are Olympic luge racing sleds." He pointed. "That one was raced in the 1988 Calgary Olympics. That one in the 1992 Albertville Olympics. That one in the 2002 Salt Lake City Olympics and that one in the 2010 Vancouver Olympics."

Johnny looked back and forth between the sleds. "No joke?"

Dmitry got serious and said, "I would never joke about something like that." He shook his head, paused, then pointed to the corner. "See that one? See how it's almost a foot longer and has a differently-shaped seat?

"That's a doubles luge sled from the 1960s. It wasn't ever raced in the Olympics, but it has the best story of all the sleds here. You see, looks can be deceiving."

15

"Wow... This place is amazing," he wrinkled his nose "But you all really need to do something about the lighting. Those four lamps on the wall don't even match."

Dmitry pressed his lips in annoyance. "There you go again – you're being confidently ignorant. You need to nip that bad habit in the bud; it's only hurting you. Why can't you just ask, 'How come those four lamps are different from each other?' Work on your humbleness. Nobody likes a know-it-all."

There it was: the hundredth person to use that phrase. Perhaps Dmitry was right, Johnny thought. He put his hands together and bent forward in a mocking half bow. "Mr. Dmitry, how come those four lamps are different? Why don't they match?"

"That's better. You know, you might actually learn something from asking questions." Dmitry flashed a big smile and said, "It's a people-skills thing...

"To answer your question, those are genuine Olympic Torches. That one's from the Los Angeles 1984 Olympics, that one from Salt Lake City 2002, that one from Torino 2006, and the last one's from Vancouver 2010. We could have bought four matching ones, but we prefer collecting different ones." Dmitry smiled and winked.

"Olympic luge sleds... Olympic Torches... Cafe Olympia. It's coming together."

Then Johnny noticed that, in addition to the framed quotes, the walls were covered with vintage photographs from the Olympics. There were even floor-to-ceiling, glass-covered bookcases filled with books.

"Dmitry, I get the Olympic pictures on the walls, but what about all the framed quotes and sayings? How do they fit in?"

"Ahhhh! A question! Much better, Grasshopper. You're learning. I'm proud of you!" he joked.

Johnny smiled and took a sip of his espresso as Dmitry leaned in further to explain how the ancient Olympics had taken place on Mt. Olympus in Greece. In Greek mythology, he said, the Greek gods were supposed to represent the highest personal development of man, and they lived in Olympia.

"My partners and I have been students of success all our lives," Dmitry continued. "We realized that, as beautiful as the Cafe Olympia building is, as good as our coffee is, and as unique as the Olympic sleds and torches are, the best way to make Cafe Olympia a special place would be to make it one where people could learn how to achieve their goals and dreams. At Cafe Olympia, we want to help people win the Gold Medal in life."

Johnny's eyes widened. *So, that's why Pablo wanted me to come here?* he thought.

"See those bookcases?" Dmitry stood up straight "They're filled with history, philosophy, and personal development books and the biographies of the most successful people in history. Those books have the distilled wisdom of the ages."

Just then, Johnny noticed an older man talking, his "students" hanging on his every word. Most of them were taking notes, and a couple were recording him with their phones.

"Who's that man sitting in the corner by the books?" he asked.

"That's RG. He's the one who raced all those sleds in the Olympics."

Johnny's shoulders dropped as he slowly exhaled "Wow."

17

"RG is a bestselling author. Companies from around the world bring him in to teach their people how to achieve their goals faster."

"No kidding." He fixed his gaze on RG.

"But RG's heart is in helping young professionals like you. Whenever he's in town, that's where you'll find him – teaching and mentoring people."

That bit of information definitely intrigued Johnny. He may come across as arrogant and a "know-it-all," as people liked reminding him, but what he wouldn't give to have a mentor like RG!

"What would I have to do to meet him?" he asked eagerly.

"Come here after five PM, and you can probably have RG to yourself." Dmitry paused, held up a finger, and said, "But before you do that, would you like a tip?"

"Yes, please – I don't want to be one of those ripe, rotting guys anymore if I can help it," Johnny smiled.

Dmitry got serious and locked his eyes on Johnny's. "RG and I believe that knowledge is not power; *applied* knowledge is power. The best way to impress RG is to implement whatever he teaches you right away with no excuses. Take consistent and persistent action. He's the leader. The fastest way to move forward in life, the shortcut, if you will, is to follow the leader."

"Thanks, Dmitry. I'll see you at five," he looked at his watch and winced inwardly at the hour–hand. "Time for me to get to work."

How to Cross a Minefield

Back at work, Johnny felt a lot better than he did the day before. The thought that somewhere in Cafe Olympia, he might find the key to turning his region around gave him hope. Even though he was only working a half day, his eyes were drawn to the clock every few minutes. He licked his lips in anticipation. He couldn't wait for 5:00 PM.

After making a list of his region's pros and cons, he was no closer to a solution than before. There were no obvious weaknesses in his team – everyone was talented, focused, and hard-working. They had all the resources they needed to do their jobs. He slowly shook his head. It was a mystery why they weren't producing nearly as much as the other regions.

With the problems at work circling his mind, at 5:00, Johnny made a bee-line for Cafe Olympia. It was buzzing like usual.

"Hi, Carl; staying busy?" Johnny greeted.

"Always!"

"Where's Dmitry?" he asked, looking around for him.

"He's usually home by now. What can I get you?"

"I had the double espresso this morning," he smiled "Why don't you surprise me this time?"

Johnny peered around the café and saw RG sitting in what he assumed must be his usual chair, reading a book. "Hang on, Carl – what's RG's usual drink?"

"He's a four-shot espresso macchiato man."

"Macchiato?"

"Macchiato means 'stained' in Italian. An espresso macchiato is 'stained' with a tablespoon of foamed milk on top."

Johnny nodded, thinking. "That sounds good. If you would, please make one for RG and one for me." He raised his hand. "But only two shots in mine. I don't think I'm ready for a four-shot espresso yet," he grinned.

"You got it. I'll call you when it's ready – you're number 11 in line."

While Johnny waited for his coffee, he walked over to the doubles luge sled leaning into the corner to get a good look at it. He peered around to make sure no one was looking and carefully lifted it up. It was a lot heavier and much more solid than the Flexible Flyer sleds he'd slid on when he was a kid. This sled was built to withstand high-speed crashes. It wasn't built for comfort; it was built for speed. It was built to get a specific job done – win races.

Johnny dropped his head and swallowed nervously. *Am I built to do what I have to do?* he thought. *Do I have what it takes to turn my region around?*

He lifted his head and read some of the quotes on the walls.

"Do what you can with what you have right now."

Teddy Roosevelt

"A good plan, violently executed now,
is better than a perfect plan next week."

General George Patton

Don't try to be perfect.
Perfectionists never get anything done
because they wait for everything to be perfect
before taking action. Nothing will ever be perfect.
Start right now. Do it now!

Johnny rubbed his chin. These people really value taking action, he mused.

If you want to succeed fast, be willing to fail fast.
If you want to succeed big, be willing to fail big.

Don't waste your failures. Find the lesson and move on.

"Valentine! Your order's ready," called out Carl.

Johnny adjusted his tie and jacket, picked up the two espressos, took a deep breath, and walked over to RG.

He was reading a big book when Johnny walked up and asked, "Mr. RG, may I join you?"

"Sure, sit down," the man smiled, placing a bookmark in between the crisp white pages and setting the book on the table in front of him. Johnny placed RG's coffee next to it and sat down. "Four-shot espresso macchiato."

RG nodded. "Thank you," he said politely. "You did your homework. I'm impressed." He took a sip of his espresso and said, "Mmm... No one makes a better espresso than Carl. We're blessed to have him on our team. So, what's your name?"

21

"Johnny Valentine," he offered, casting his eyes around for an interesting point of discussion. His gaze finally fell on RG's book. "What are you reading?" he asked.

"This is one of the finest biographies of Napoleon Bonaparte," RG explained, caressing the book's spine. "I'm hoping to discover some leadership insights."

"Have you learned anything interesting?"

RG nodded pensively before telling Johnny he'd discovered that, before becoming a great leader, Napoleon was first a great follower. He always had a deep hunger that drove him to learn from other leaders. He was a leadership sponge.

"The rest is history," RG finished.

Johnny wrinkled his forehead. "I never thought of Napoleon as a follower, but the way you explain it makes a lot of sense."

"Every great leader was first a great follower," explained RG. "That's true in every field – sports, business, military, politics, education, etcetera. It's just a Principle of Success."

"Principle of Success?" Johnny questioned, leaning in; he knew he was about to hear some true wisdom, and he didn't want to miss anything.

"A Principle of Success is a rule that works for anyone, anywhere, anytime." RG took another sip of his coffee. "Tell me, Johnny, what brings you to Cafe Olympia?"

Johnny looked down. On the one hand, he wanted to keep his problems to himself – his arrogant, egotistical side, no doubt – but he also knew that he'd be failing himself if he didn't open up with RG. "I've been struggling at work, and my boss suggested I come here," he finally explained. "He said I just might find the key to solving my challenge."

"Interesting... What do you do?"

"I'm a regional manager at Garcia Munos IT Services."

"Pablo Garcia Munos's business!" RG said excitedly.

Johnny raised his eyebrows. "Do you know Pablo?"

"Everybody in business knows Pablo and his inspiring business story."

Johnny had no idea what RG was talking about, but he pretended that he knew. "Yes, I guess so."

"What's your challenge at work?"

And before he knew it, Johnny was spilling all the pent-up frustration he'd been feeling for the past few months. He told RG how he'd been working for Pablo for nine months, and throughout all those months, his region had been in last place in production. He fidgeted and pulled at his collar. "Yesterday, Pablo warned me that unless I turned my region around by the end of this quarter, I won't have a job anymore," he finished.

"Hmm... That doesn't sound like Pablo... Did he offer to help you out?"

"Yes," he nodded. "Both Pablo and Linda, the VP of Sales, offered to help me, but I told them that I had it under control." His eyes narrowed, and he tilted his head. "That's when Pablo gave me his ultimatum."

"I see."

He pressed on. "At the end of the day, I asked Pablo if he had any ideas. That's when he suggested that I come here. I was here this morning – Dmitry showed me around and told me Cafe Olympia's story and about you."

RG smiled. "And how can I serve you, Johnny?"

Johnny shrugged and shook his head. "I'm not sure. I don't even know where to start. I'm stumped. I graduated with honors from Wharton with two MBAs. My team is strong. We have plenty of resources. We work hard. Yet, we've been in last place out of our five regions ever since I've been here."

RG pointed to a bookcase. "Johnny, would you mind reading out what's on the picture frame on the top shelf?"

Johnny did so with relish. "'If you have to cross a minefield, it makes sense to follow someone who's already crossed it.'"

"What does that mean to you, Johnny?"

Johnny shrugged his shoulders. "Sounds like some practical military wisdom."

"When I was growing up, my dad used to say that to me all the time. And he didn't even serve in the military." RG pointed to the framed saying, "Here's what that saying means. Find someone who's already done what you want to do, and follow in their footsteps. Find a coach or mentor who's been in the trenches and has fruit on the trees – results. Following the leader is the fastest and easiest way to achieve any goal. Following the leader is the shortcut to success."

Johnny frowned. "I wouldn't even know who to ask."

"Someone who's already done what you want to do. Think about it – who's the top regional manager in your company? Who's in first place most of the time?"

"Bob Hall," Johnny spat out immediately and rolled his eyes, snorting. "But he didn't even go to business school."

If you have to cross a minefield, it makes sense to follow someone who's already crossed it.

"Johnny, don't get caught up with degrees and things like how many letters a person has after their name." RG clenched his jaw. "Education's a great thing, but the acid test is this… are they getting results?" RG had a point, Johnny thought. Bill Gates, Steve Jobs, and Michael Dell never finished college, but they had done okay, right? "Sounds to me like Bob Hall might be able to help you out," RG added.

Johnny crossed his arms and shook his head. "But he's so busy. I wouldn't want to impose."

"Have you ever heard people say that successful people are seldom fulfilled or satisfied?"

"Yes, I have."

"You know why? Because success isn't the Gold Medal. Most people think it is, but it's not; it's the Silver Medal. You know what the Gold Medal is?"

Johnny shook his head.

"Significance. You achieve significance by helping someone else succeed. You get it by creating a ripple effect of success. By making a difference in someone else's life. By making the world a better place. Significance is the Gold Medal." He slowly exhaled and relaxed. "That's why I spend all my free time here, helping people like you."

"Hmm, I never thought about it that way, but it makes sense," Johnny reasoned, taking a sip of his macchiato; he had to admit that it was quite delicious.

"Johnny, as long as you're willing to wholeheartedly take action on whatever Bob Hall says you need to do to improve your region's results, you owe it to him to ask for help."

Johnny's eyes widened. "I owe it to HIM?"

"Yes," RG reasoned, ignoring Johnny's reaction entirely. "He'll help you get your Silver Medal and keep your job, and you'll help him get his Gold Medal, making a difference."

By this point, Johnny was leaning forward and looking intently at RG.

"Mentorship is a two-way street," RG continued. Johnny contemplated noting all this down in his phone, but he didn't want to appear too eager. "The mentor's job is to teach and correct and encourage. The mentee's job is to be a good follower. To follow the mentor's advice by taking action right away. The same is true in the coach/athlete relationship. If both of you do your job, the team has a better chance to win."

Johnny sat up straight and held out his hand. "Mr. RG, thank you for your time and for helping me understand these success principles. Would it be okay to meet with you again?"

"We're just laying down a foundation for success. We'll have to meet many times for you to learn even the basics." RG paused. "Johnny, listen very carefully to what I'm going to tell you."

RG took a long, slow sip from his cup to make sure Johnny was paying attention. He maintained steady eye contact with Johnny and pointed his finger at him. "I only work with people who are hungry and who follow my advice right away. I only work with action people. So, make sure to act on the things I teach you.

Find the right leader –
someone who's already done
what you want to do.

"Remember, action produces confidence. Inaction strengthens fear. Every time you take a risk, you expand your comfort zone. Always do the thing that scares you most. All the best things in life are on the other side of that fear."

Johnny eyed RG curiously.

"Just think about when you were a kid on the high dive in your neighborhood pool – the longer you waited to dive, the worse the fear got. But once you decided to dive, the fear went away, and you spent the rest of the afternoon diving. Taking action made it fun. Taking action made it exhilarating."

Johnny's mouth was slightly open as he felt fear rise up. "What if I fail?" he voiced nervously.

RG stuck his chest out and pounded his fist on the table "If you fail, you take the lesson, and you'll be further ahead than if you hadn't done anything. The only time you should be afraid to fail is the last time you're willing to try."

Johnny's eyes were wide open; an entirely new world had just revealed itself in front of him. RG continued, "Failure is a stepping stone to success. Most people never win because they are afraid of losing. Attack your fears. If you don't, you'll be their servant for the rest of your life."

RG swiftly finished his drink and stood. Johnny took that as an invitation to leave and followed suit. "Think about what we talked about and act on it," RG advised. "Only then will I agree to meet with you again. You know where to find me. Good luck, and I hope to see you soon."

"Thanks again, RG," Johnny replied, shaking RG's hand enthusiastically. "I'll get to work."

Find Your Leader

The meeting with RG had gone nothing like what Johnny had expected. He had meant to ask him about the Olympics, but since RG got right into teaching him about the mine field and taking action, he never got a chance to ask.

On the way back home, Johnny's head was spinning. He was grateful for the opportunity to meet with RG, and he realized that he needed to earn the privilege to meet with him again.

Despite his failings, Johnny needed to admit that he had them – and that someone as successful as Bob Hall could actually help him. He just needed to bite the bullet and call. As soon as Johnny got home, he mustered up the courage to ring Bob. "Bob, this is Johnny Valentine. Sorry to bother you after work. Do you have a minute?"

"Sure, Johnny; how can I help?" Bob replied.

"Is there any chance we could meet sometime tomorrow? Maybe even for coffee in the morning? I'm in trouble at work, and I really need to pick your brain."

Johnny told Bob about how he needed to turn his region around and thought that if anyone could help him, it was Bob.

"Absolutely," Bob happily stated. "I'm honored that you think I might be able to help out. Coffee at 7:00 tomorrow morning works for me. Where do you want to meet?"

"Ever been to Cafe Olympia?"

"Never heard of it."

They agreed to meet there; Johnny quickly gave him the address. "You're not going to believe this café. My treat. And thanks!"

"Terrific. Let's make the most out of our time. Why don't you bring a list of questions for me? It'll give us a place to get started. See you tomorrow."

Johnny was in Cafe Olympia at 6:30 AM – he wanted to make sure he could find an open table and have a chance to go over his questions one more time before Bob Hall got there.

Dmitry was chatting with Carl, and RG was already surrounded by a group of mentees.

Bob Hall arrived at 6:45 and spotted Johnny. "Early bird, huh?" he smiled.

"Dad always said that the early bird gets the worm," Johnny grinned by way of greeting.

"Your dad was a smart man," Bob said, eyeing up the café's interior. "Geez... you weren't kidding. This place is amazing. Thanks for suggesting it."

Johnny was excited. "It's a really special place. Pablo told me about it. Wait till you taste the coffee..."

Bernie, the waiter, came up to their table and asked them what they'd like.

They both ordered, then Johnny immediately pulled out a legal pad with his questions; he didn't want to waste any time. He asked Bob where he'd learned to run a region the way he did and how he went about it. Bob showed Johnny how he organized his workload, prioritized his time, and used specific indicators to always know where he needed to focus next.

Johnny was amazed; Bob ran his region completely differently than he did. Not only was he able to stay ahead of the eight ball, but most of the time, he could predict where future challenges might be lurking. Thanks to his systems, Bob was never reactive like Johnny always was.

Instead, most of the time, Bob could be proactive and take advantage of opportunities.

Like RG had said, degrees didn't have anything to do with it – Bob Hall had elegant systems in place that helped him to be more efficient, effective, and productive. Like Johnny, Bob worked very hard, but thanks to his systems, he could work smart too.

"I've always been amazed at how you're consistently able to get great results," Johnny beamed. "Now I see how you do it. I'm humbled and thankful that you would share your systems with me." He looked down and paused for a moment. "Bob, I don't know how to thank you."

"Here's how you can thank me," Bob replied. "By implementing everything that I just taught you right away, and by having your best quarter ever. Johnny," he added, "you don't have any time to waste. You have to make major changes, and you'd better do them quickly – or else."

"How long do you think it will take to start seeing results?" he replied anxiously – evidently, anything he put in place needed a quick outcome. It was his job on the line, after all.

"Even if you start using my systems today, it might take as long as two months for you to start seeing any results," Bob explained to a crest-fallen Johnny; he didn't expect miracles, and while two months could work, it seemed like an awfully long time to him. "Have faith, work your tail off, and remember – I'm a phone call away if you have any questions."

"Thanks, Bob."

Bob leaned forward and put his hand on Johnny's shoulder. "Make me proud, Johnny. And thanks for telling me about this place. I'm going to start coming here. What a great place to bring clients."

Johnny couldn't wait to get to work. As soon as he got there, he called an emergency meeting for all his managers. "Guys, I need to apologize to all of you because I've failed you."

The managers looked at each other, then stared at Johnny with wide eyes. They were shocked to hear Johnny apologize for anything; he was not the apologizing kind. He was overconfident, arrogant, brash, and sometimes even cocky.

"You're a great team. Knowledgeable, focused, and hard-working. But ever since I came here, we haven't had a single good quarter. But that's about to change." Johnny rubbed his hands together and smiled.

"This morning, I met with Bob Hall. As you know, Bob's region has been number one in production for the last seven quarters in a row. I asked him for help, and he was gracious enough to share with me some of the things they do to consistently get great results."

He tightened his fists and stood confident and tall "Starting today, we're going to run our region exactly like Bob runs his. We'll be using the same systems Bob uses. We'll still work hard, but we're going to start getting better results from our effort."

He held up his palms. "I ask you to have faith in me. Have faith in Bob's systems. Work as hard as you always work, and hopefully, in eight to ten weeks, we'll start seeing better results.

"Our region has been holding the whole company back," he added, careful not to bring the hammer down too harshly. "If we're able to turn our region around, the overall company profits will increase dramatically. When that happens, I'll ask Pablo for some kind of special reward for us."

Johnny lifted his finger and shook it at his team. "Remember, the battle goes to those who act with faith and bravery and who persevere. The harder the struggle, the more glorious the triumph. I believe in you. Let's win together!"

As Johnny was talking, he could see a transformation in his managers. First, they started straightening up in their chairs, then they began to lean forward, slowly nod their heads, and finally stand and gave Johnny a round of applause.

Johnny walked to the door and encouraged each of his managers personally as they left the conference room and headed back to work. He shook each of their hands and either hugged or patted them on the back as they exited.

"I believe in you, Pete."

"Together, we can do this, Vicky."

"DJ, I'm proud to work with you."

"We can do this, Steve."

"I appreciate you, Lauren."

After the last person left the conference room, Johnny took a deep breath, looked up, closed his eyes, and slowly exhaled. Smiling, he felt hopeful that they would turn their region around.

The shortcut to achieving your goals faster is to follow the leader's advice right away.

Unlikely Olympian

Johnny was so busy getting the new systems into place that he forgot about Cafe Olympia for two days. On the third day, he went back after work.

"Hi, Carl, how you been?" he greeted.

"Doing fine, Johnny. Where have you been? Business trip?"

"No, just very busy at work. Exciting stuff..." he trailed, reminiscing on all the great work his team had done so far. It was very early days, but momentum was already building in his very bones. He quickly ordered two espressos – one four-shot and the other two – and wandered off to look at some of the pictures on the wall.

There were images of athletes marching in the Olympic Opening Ceremonies, photos of luge athletes competing, and pictures of athletes standing proudly on the medal podiums. There were also images of athletes working on their sleds, eating together, and even of them traveling together in crowded vans. The more Johnny took in, the more impressed he was with Cafe Olympia.

"Valentine, order ready!"

Johnny picked up the two cups and walked over to RG's corner. He didn't need to take a deep breath like he had on the first day. In fact, he was smiling. RG was still reading the book about Napoleon. Johnny noticed he had a notebook to jot down things from his books.

"Mr. RG, may I join you?" He placed RG's espresso in front of him.

"Absolutely. Sit down. Thanks for the espresso – you're too kind," he nodded.

"My pleasure, RG – it's the least I can do," he smiled. "I give you a little bit of coffee, and you give me priceless advice."

RG laughed. "I haven't seen you lately. Have you been okay?"

"Better than okay."

"Actually, I saw you a couple of mornings ago, sitting at a table with someone else. That wouldn't have been Bob Hall by any chance, would it?"

"It was," Johnny nodded. He told RG how he'd approached Bob, like he'd suggested, and that he was teaching Johnny the systems he used in his region to consistently get stellar results. "I've been so busy implementing Bob's systems in my region that I haven't had a chance to come here," he finished.

RG grinned from ear to ear. "Wonderful! I'm proud of you. You're following the leader! Only one out of ten of my students acts on my advice so quickly. So… are you seeing any progress?"

"We may not see progress for eight to ten weeks, Johnny explained. "But we have faith that if it worked for Bob, it will work for us," he smiled.

RG nodded. "That's a great attitude to have – delayed gratification. Long-term thinking. Being willing to continue doing the right things with faith that the results will come. You're trying to turn a big ship around. And that takes time."

Johnny listened, sipping his delicious coffee – that was quickly becoming his new favorite – as RG told him that it was human nature to want immediate gratification, to want everything right now. "Those people never succeed," he said. "They're the people who go to the gym or stick with a diet for a week, look in the mirror, then quit because they don't look any fitter."

When Pablo had first called Johnny up to his office, it had occurred to Johnny that he should just quit – but Pablo's belief in him and offering to help quickly dismissed that thought.

"Success takes time," RG continued. "It takes delayed gratification and long-term thinking. Long-term thinking helps you make better decisions today. Johnny," he pressed, looking at him from across the table, "you're on the right track. Make sure to teach your managers these things so that everyone's on the same page. If you can create a culture of delayed gratification, the sky's the limit."

Johnny was busy taking notes – no longer concerned with how eager this would make him look. He didn't want to forget any of RG's nuggets.

"You know what? I did see a change in my managers. They're really excited about the new systems, and it almost feels like they respect me more for asking Bob for help than they did when I tried to do everything on my own."

"Wonderful. Why do you think they respect you more now?"

Johnny shrugged. He really didn't know. He told RG that he'd always tried to be strong and in control and have all the answers for them. The one time he was weak and had to ask for answers, he got more respect. "It doesn't make sense to me."

RG shook his head. "Johnny, you have it all wrong – that's why it doesn't make sense to you. When you try to be in control and have all the answers, you're being weak. You're being fake. When you let go, get real, realize you don't have all the answers, and look for them outside of yourself, you're being strong. That's why you're getting more respect. Because you're letting go, you're being real and doing what's best for the team, not just what you think will make you look good."

Johnny listened and tried to make sense of what RG was saying; his advice seemed spot-on.

"You're on the right track." RG took a sip of his coffee "So, how can I help you today?"

Johnny looked about, then pointed to the things around him. "RG, I've never been to a place like Cafe Olympia. The history, the luge sleds, the Olympic Torches, the pictures and quotes on the walls. The book collection. It's actually a bit overwhelming. And you being an Olympian amazes me. I've never met an Olympian before."

RG listened intently as Johnny carried on, enthused.

"Dmitry told me the story of how Cafe Olympia came to be. Would you tell me how you became an Olympian? Maybe I can learn some success principles from your journey."

RG frowned and crossed his arms. "Okay, but you need to take me off that pedestal – I'm no good to you up there. High achievers are ordinary people who have an extraordinary dream, a burning desire to achieve it, and the willingness to do whatever it takes for as long as it takes to get the job done."

The simple truth was, Olympians all followed the same success principles – following the right coach or mentor, getting started, and refusing to quit on the way to their dream. "Anyone can realize their goals and dreams by following the same principles," he explained.

"So, how did you get started?" Johnny pressed.

"I was born in Argentina. Our family moved to the States when I was six years old. School was tough for me because I was the only kid in my class who didn't speak English."

Johnny listened intently as RG explained how he'd always loved reading, particularly adventure books, like *Around the World in 80 Days, 20,000 Leagues Under the Sea*, and all of Jules Verne's books about kids who lead adventurous lives.

"We had the books in Spanish and in English," he added. "My parents hired an English tutor, and slowly but surely, I learned how to speak English."

Find the right leader,
follow the leader right away,
get started, and don't quit.

RG took a sip of his coffee before continuing; he quite liked returning to his childhood and remembering how he'd grown up in the world.

He wanted his life to be an adventure, just like the kids in the books he read. "I was always looking for my adventure," he said. "When I was ten years old, I saw the Olympics on TV for the first time. I turned to my younger brother Marcelo and said, 'The Olympics! That's my adventure! I'll be an Olympian!'

"That's when I caught the dream. But it was a pipe dream because I didn't think it was possible."

"Why didn't you think it was possible?" Johnny asked, completely invested.

"Well, you'd expect an Olympian to be a great athlete, right?"

Johnny nodded. "Of course. The best!"

"Well, let's just say that I'm an unlikely Olympian."

"What do you mean?"

RG shrugged then raised his palms. "I can't run fast, I can't jump high, and I'm not very strong. I'm like your neighbor. All throughout school, I was the last kid picked to play sports in PE. Believe it or not, I was on the bench for kickball. I didn't even know they had a bench in kickball!"

Johnny frowned.

There were always two team captains choosing teams, RG explained. The last team captain always said the same thing: "I have to get RG again?" RG found it very frustrating and didn't play sports in middle school or high school.

Johnny held his hands up and motioned for RG to stop, "Wait a minute. I don't get it – you weren't a great athlete, and you competed in four Winter Olympics? That doesn't make any sense."

"It's definitely uncommon. Did you play sports in school?"

Johnny dropped his head and rubbed his hair, slowly shaking his head back and forth. "RG, my sports story is exactly the opposite of yours."

"What do you mean?"

"I was blessed with speed, agility, and strength" I had so much natural athletic ability that I was always the first kid picked for sports." In fact, Johnny hadn't even had to try. He'd played organized sports in middle school and in high school, lettering in baseball, football, and basketball. "I expected to get a full-ride scholarship in baseball at the college of my choice, but I wasn't even recruited. I never played college sports. I still can't understand why."

He clenched his fists. "Talk about frustrating. I'm 27, and it still bugs me today." He cursed under his breath.

"Interesting. Opposite stories, but we were both frustrated."

Johnny crossed his arms, then violently gestured with his arm. "Yeah, but you got to go to the Olympics... Incredible!" He paused and shook his head, repeating, "Incredible."

"Johnny, frustration's not fun, but it's not a bad thing," RG reasoned. "It means you care. Take advantage of your frustration. Use it to get mad, then to go from anger to determination and finally to taking bold action."

Johnny nodded, paying close attention. He wrote "Frustration => Anger => Determination => Action," down on his notepad.

"So, you played sports in high school – where was that?" RG asked.

"Vince Lombardi High, here in town."

"Really? Was Matt Phillips your baseball coach?"

"Yes, he was. I can't believe he's still coaching. You know him?"

"We've known each other for years. Matt's a fine man." He leaned forward. "You know he played pro baseball in Europe, right?"

"No." Johnny crinkled his nose and creased his brow. "I can't believe he never mentioned it."

"That's Matt's style. He's always been very low-key."

Johnny quickly changed the subject; he disliked not being in the know – something that would no doubt change the more he spoke to RG. "So, how did you get to the Olympics? Now I'm more curious than ever."

"Like I said, I caught the dream, but I didn't take action because I didn't believe it was possible. But I was so fascinated with the Olympics that I wouldn't stop talking about it. The funny thing is that what drew me to the

41

Olympic athletes wasn't their athleticism – it was their spirit." RG's eyes widened.

Johnny tilted his head. "Their spirit?"

"Yes. Right away, I saw that this was a group of people who had a dream, and they were going to go for it no matter what. They were willing to train for years and years with no guarantees of success." He nodded slightly and smiled. "They became my heroes, and I wanted to be like them."

After a couple of years, RG explained, his dad had gotten tired of hearing him talk the talk but not walk the walk. "My dad told me I should read some biographies. That if I studied the lives of great people, I'd discover what works and what doesn't work in life because success leaves clues."

Johnny wrinkled his forehead. "Success leaves clues? What do you mean?"

"It means you don't have to make all the mistakes. You can learn from other people's mistakes."

"Oh." He nodded; things were starting to make much more sense the more he spent time with RG; the man really was an inspiration.

"So," RG continued, sipping his drink, "I started reading biographies, and I liked them right away because they were true-life adventures." After a while, RG had noticed that every biography was basically the same story. It was the story of someone who had a dream, went through a struggle, and then had their victory. "It was always dream, struggle, victory," RG added.

"Then I started looking for something all these people had in common, something I could try to develop in myself. You know what I kept seeing over and over again?"

Johnny shrugged and shook his head.

"Perseverance. They refused to give up. They were a bunch of hardheads. My mom always called me a hardhead, so I thought, 'Maybe I have a little bit of what it takes.'" RG winked and smiled.

"That's funny."

"Some of these people I read about banged their heads on the wall for 20 years. But if they didn't quit, one of two things always happened."

Johnny raised his eyebrows, intrigued.

"They either figured it out on their own through sheer trial-and-error, or else they ran into someone who'd already done what they wanted to do, and that person became their coach or mentor. Their leader."

This was really interesting to Johnny. It sometimes felt that RG was hearing his very thoughts. "It's funny you should say that," he voiced, "because I'm starting to think Pablo had me come to Cafe Olympia because he thought I might find a mentor here." He fell silent.

"Maybe..." RG nodded wisely. "But think about this: coming here helped you find a mentor at work – Bob Hall."

Johnny's jaw dropped. "Wow, I hadn't thought of that." He paused, "It's pretty incredible when you think about it."

"It's not so incredible to me," RG smiled over the edge of his coffee cup.

Johnny tilted his head. "It's not?"

"No," he continued, placing the empty cup on the table; Johnny watched the coffee remnants slide to the bottom. "When the student is ready, the teacher will appear," RG explained. "You're in a receptive state of mind right now, so you're able to learn from others. The key is to stay in that humble, hungry, willing to learn state of mind."

"Green and growing! Like Dmitry says," Johnny nodded.

"Exactly. Always green and growing. Not ripe and rotting."

"So, what happened after you read the biographies?"

When RG was only 12 years old, he had made a decision that changed his life. He decided that if perseverance was the key to achieving your dreams, he wouldn't quit anything anymore. "Not quitting doesn't guarantee you'll win, but you still have a chance," he told Johnny. "You're still in the game. As long as you don't quit, there's still hope. If you quit, it's all over."

RG had realized that if he started quitting everything he started, quitting would become a bad habit, and he would never achieve his dreams. "The thought of that was so scary to me that it was easy for me to persevere."

RG swirled the last of the coffee around his cup, thinking. "By high school, my nickname was Bulldog. Other kids noticed that I was tenacious and perseverant. Now, I had to live up to my nickname, and that made me even more perseverant."

"You created positive peer pressure!" Johnny smiled.

"Ha, ha, that's good… I guess I did."

Johnny tilted his head. "So, that was it? Your perseverance got you to the Olympics?"

"No, that was just part of it. My dad always said, 'The books you read and the people you associate with will determine if you achieve your dreams.'"

Johnny nodded. "I think I've heard that before."

"I'm sure you have. It's been around forever. Benjamin Franklin used to call it cherry-picking." When picking a cherry from a cherry tree, you don't pick a green one – you pick the ripest, sweetest ones, RG explained. "Benjamin Franklin would pick the best characteristics from successful people and try to develop them in himself."

Johnny listened intently as RG told him that you become like the people you associate with because you pick up their habits. That was why it was important to associate with people he had respect for. People who got things done, who had already done what he wanted to do. Successful people.

"Successful people think big," RG noted, watching Johnny scrawl more notes on his pad. "They think and talk about what they want. They focus on the dream, not on the obstacles. There will always be obstacles, but they always focus on the dream."

"Why?" asked Johnny.

"Because the dream gives you strength." He pumped his fist. "It gives you the power to overcome your obstacles. Desire for a dream gives you the power to stay in the game long enough to develop the skills you'll need to achieve it.

Successful people asked themselves different questions than average people, RG explained. Questions like, "Why not me? Why not now? Why not?" "Those are great questions to ask yourself," he told Johnny. "They get your subconscious mind working on finding a way. Then you find yourself waking up in the middle of the night with ideas, solutions, and ways to reach your goals."

Johnny nodded; this all made perfect sense. Why was he only learning this now?

"Think about this, Johnny: every company and organization of consequence has a board of directors. A group of advisors. You need to have a board of directors too. A group of successful people you can go to when you need advice or an opinion on something you may be planning to do. A group of people who hold your feet to the fire, who you become accountable to. You know what I call mine?" he asked.

Johnny shook his head.

"My Dream Team – because they help me achieve my dreams." He raised his eyebrows and smiled.

Johnny smiled back. "I like that. Your own Dream Team."

"But that's not all your Dream Team helps you do. They help you get through your struggles."

Johnny's smile faded.

RG leaned forward, suddenly seeming more serious. "I've got news for you, Johnny: you're going to have bad days. You'll have bad weeks. You will have bad months. Once in a while, you'll even have a bad year." God knows RG had. There were years when it seemed that no matter how hard he worked, nothing worked out, times when he questioned and doubted himself, when he was so discouraged, all he wanted to do was quit.

Johnny leaned in.

"Thank God that I latched on to my Coach's belief in me when I didn't believe in myself," RG said. "Thank God that I listened when Coach explained to me that, even though I wasn't getting the results I wanted, I was gaining experience and growing into the type of person who'd get those results down the road. Thank God that I listened to Coach. Because he could see further than I could, and he was a constant source of power and strength."

"I hadn't thought about it that way. Your Coach and your Dream Team were like a support system."

"Many times, they were like a lifeline that kept me from drowning."

"Wow." Johnny's eyes widened, then he looked down.

RG explained with a story, "I have a good friend who's a world-class aerobatic pilot and wing walker. Karen Peña's dad started teaching her to fly when she was six years old."

"I don't think I was even riding a bike when I was six!" exclaimed Johnny.

Flying had become Karen's passion, and her dad had always surrounded her with people who could become her mentors – her Dream Team. Years later, Karen was going to compete against the best pilots in America at the National Aerobatics Championships.

RG continued, "A couple of days before the competition, a rumor started that a very famous actor, someone Karen admired, had just signed up to compete in her category. Everyone was buzzing about the news."

"Who was it?"

"If I told you, you wouldn't believe me. Anyways, Karen was one of the favorites," RG made flying motions with his hand, "but she lost her focus and started making amateur mistakes in her flying."

Johnny put his coffee cup down and leaned forward.

"Right away, she called PJ, one of her Dream Team friends on the phone. PJ said, 'Karen, you need to get that out of your head right now. Get that handsome actor out of your head. Picture that an ugly dude's flying that plane.'"

Johnny laughed out loud.

RG went on, "PJ said it was just a hobby for him. 'Flying is your life,' she said, 'and this is your year. Don't look at him and don't get pictures with him. He should want his picture with you, because you will be the champion!'"

"Karen followed PJ's advice and went on to win the National Aerobatic Championship."

"Wow! How'd the actor do?"

"He didn't even show up at the championship!"

"What?"

"He had to do a last-minute re-shoot for another movie."

RG pointed at Johnny, "But here's the point. The rumor

unfocused Karen and almost cost her the championship. It's a good thing that as soon as she was in trouble, she reached out to her Dream Team for advice."

Johnny exhaled slowly as he nodded his head in understanding.

Sensing the change in tension, RG asked, "How about you, Johnny? What do you do when the going gets tough? When life hits you with storms? Do you try to figure it out on your own?"

Johnny stuck his chest out and pushed his shoulders back, trying to appear confident. "I've always prided myself on being self-sufficient and self-reliant."

RG frowned, then motioned with his hands. "What about when you can't find the answer? Then what? Do you start feeling sorry for yourself? Do you go out and have a pity party? Do you start blaming circumstances instead of taking responsibility? Do you get frustrated, then discouraged to the point where you quit?"

Johnny remained silent; good questions, he thought.

"The next time you're in the middle of one of life's storms, the next time you're discouraged and starting to doubt yourself, don't try to figure it out on your own. The worst time to make an important decision is when things aren't going your way."

Johnny leaned forward and slowly nodded his head.

RG continued, "If you do that, you'll be basing your decision entirely on emotion, not on intellect. If you make a decision when you're down, you're bound to make a bad one because you'll be tempted to take the easy way out. That's when you're the closest to quitting.

"When things aren't going your way. Pick up the phone. Call your best friend, your coach, your mentor, or your boss – your leader. Call someone who cares for you, someone who believes in you, someone who'll get you back on track and won't let you quit. Because if you quit on your dream, you'll regret it all your life. Guaranteed."

Johnny nodded again, deeply immersed in his note-taking.

RG picked up a Bible lying on his table. "Have you ever heard of the Book of Proverbs?"

"Dmitry was telling me about it the other day," Johnny admitted. "That's the one that was written by a smart, rich guy, right?"

"That's right, King Solomon." RG nodded. "Now, listen to some of the things King Solomon wrote: 'Fools think their own way is right, but the wise listen to advice.'" RG flipped a few pages. "'Listen to advice and accept instruction, that you may gain wisdom in the future.'" He flipped a few more pages, "'Without wise counsel, a nation falls; there is safety in having many advisers.'" More page-flipping. "'Plans succeed through good counsel; don't go to war without wise advice.'" He shut the book and placed it back on the table before continuing. "Johnny, if it's good enough for kings and nations, don't you think it might be good for you and me too?"

Johnny nodded slowly, smiled, and said, "Point taken."

Associating with winners was only half of it, RG explained. People needed to disassociate from whiners, excuse-makers, and complainers. "Small-minded people," RG added. His breath quickened as he pointed to a picture on the wall. "Albert Einstein said, 'Great ideas will always be challenged by mediocre minds.'"

RG continued, "If you associate with whiners, as soon as you try to do something special, as soon as you try to break out of the pack, they'll pull you down. Small-minded people believe that your success makes them look bad.

49

They'll do anything they can to create doubt in your mind to get you to stop believing in yourself. They're dangerous because they have the power to make you quit on your dream."

"What if I try to explain my dream to them?"

RG curled his nose in disgust. "A dreamer will never be understood by a non-dreamer, so don't waste your precious energy trying to make your critics understand you. It'll never happen."

Johnny kept taking notes. He could tell RG was on a roll.

*"Fools think their own way is right,
but the wise listen to advice.
Listen to advice and accept instruction,
that you may gain wisdom in the future."*

Proverbs 12:15 & 19:20

"Johnny, do you remember Apple's famous 'Think Different' commercial? It said it best."

Johnny shook his head. "I'm not sure I remember it. Maybe it was before my time."

"It's a classic. Would you mind bringing me the framed picture with all the headshots?" He pointed to a bookcase.

Johnny put his notebook down and got the picture for RG.

RG read the quote from the 1997 Apple commercial with awe and respect. "'Here's to the crazy ones, the misfits, the rebels, the troublemakers, the round pegs in the square holes... the ones who see things differently – they're not fond of rules... You can quote them, disagree with them, glorify or vilify them, but the only thing you can't do is ignore them because they change things... they push the human race forward, and while some may see them as the crazy ones, we see genius, because the ones who are crazy enough to think that they can change the world, are the ones who do.'"

He looked up at Johnny. "Johnny, do you recognize any of the people in the headshots?"

Johnny started pointing at the headshots and naming the ones he recognized. "Sure, that's Albert Einstein, Bob Dylan, Martin Luther King, Richard Branson, John Lennon, Thomas Edison, Muhammad Ali, Gandhi, Amelia Earhart, and Alfred Hitchcock."

RG slowly named the ones Johnny could not recognize, taking the time to let every name sink in. "That's Ted Turner... Buckminster Fuller... Maria Callas... Martha Graham... Jim Henson... Frank Lloyd Wright... and Pablo Picasso.

"A lot of people didn't understand them because they were dreamers," said RG. "They were ahead of their time. Trust me – don't waste your time and energy trying to get your critics to understand you."

Johnny nodded and raised his palms. "Okay, I'll trust you on that."

RG's dad had said he'd never achieve anything great in life until he started believing that something inside him was bigger than the circumstances he faced. "The best way to do that is to force yourself to hang around successful people," RG voiced. "You'll feel awkward, you'll feel like you don't belong, you'll feel out of place, but if you do, their success thinking will rub off on you. You'll start thinking big. And when those people start believing in you, you'll start believing in yourself because you respect their opinion."

Johnny's eyes were getting wider. "So, did you do what your dad said?"

"Yes, and over a period of time, I started growing and believing more in myself." It was only then that he started facing his fears and taking bigger risks. Then, his life started to become an adventure.

"Just like the kids in the books you read," Johnny added.

"Exactly!" RG slapped the table in enthusiasm. "As long as you take action and follow the leader, the books you read and the people you associate with have the power to change your life. That's why we created Cafe Olympia."

"You're the owner?" This was news to Johnny; neither Dmitry nor Carl had mentioned this in the conversations he'd had with them about the café's history.

"I'm one of the partners," RG smiled. "I teamed up with some like-minded friends, and together, we created a special place with an environment conducive to success."

"RG, this place is amazing," Johnny enthused. "I can't believe everyone here is talking. There's not a single person working on a laptop."

"That's because there's no Wi-Fi at Cafe Olympia."

Johnny smacked his palm on his forehead. "What? No Wi-Fi? I've never heard of a coffee shop with no Wi-Fi. Isn't that bad for business?"

"Our business model is completely different from typical coffee shops." They were more like a Success University that happened to serve coffee, catering to people who wanted to learn how to develop themselves and be the best they could be.

"Bernie and Monica, our servers, keep the people at the tables moving just like waiters at a restaurant would," RG explained. "As long as our guests are eating and drinking, they're welcome to sit at a table. If they want to hang around and chat, they can stand at the bar. We even offer a 30% discount at the bar." This plan had worked out in their favor almost immediately; the last thing they wanted was for someone to order a cup of coffee and camp out at a table working for hours. "That would infuriate all the people who are waiting for a table."

Johnny creased his brow, unconvinced. "I still don't know if it's good business for you not to have Wi-Fi."

"Think about your business," RG reasoned. "You don't want *any* customer – you only want the customers who are the best fit for the products and services that you offer. Customers who appreciate the way you do business. Those customers are your fans, and they'll tell other similar people about what you offer."

Johnny cocked his head to the side, still struggling with his logic. "Hmm, I don't know about that. Right now, I'd be happy for *any* new clients."

"Here's something else," RG pressed on, ignoring Johnny's skepticism. "You only want employees who love working for you. Employees who are a good fit for their jobs. Sometimes, the reason people aren't getting great results is that they're not working in the right place. You'll always work harder and have more pride in your work if you're doing something you love."

Johnny frowned.

"I can see that you're not convinced. Run it by Bob Hall, and let me know his thoughts on this – after all, it sounds like he may be the first person in your Dream Team."

Johnny nodded; that was something he could do. "Okay, I will."

A couple of college students walked up to RG's and Johnny's table. RG greeted them warmly.

"Hi, Marcia, hello, Pete. It's so good to see you. Is it our time already?"

Marcia and Pete smiled and nodded.

RG turned to Johnny. "Johnny, I'm sorry, I have an appointment with these students. I'll tell you the rest of the story next time I see you. Let me know what Bob Hall says."

Johnny rose from his seat and, shaking RG's hand and with a quick, polite smile to the students, he left the café feeling energized and ready to take on the day.

Dream Clients

As soon as Johnny got home, he called Bob Hall. "Hi, Bob; I need to ask you for a big favor."

Johnny asked him if he'd mind coming over to the office sometime that week to look around and make sure they were doing things right. Bob was more than happy to help out, so they agreed on a time for him to visit for around 45 minutes.

That was plenty of time, Johnny reasoned. "I'll make sure all my managers are there," he explained. "I think that seeing you will have a positive impact. Plus, if anyone has questions, they can get them answered right away."

Before Bob hung up, Johnny decided to tell him about RG's advice he'd been given that day.

"He's been giving me tips that might help me with my region. In fact, he's the one who suggested I learn from whoever's region operated the best." Johnny narrowed his eyes. "He said something that didn't make sense to me, then he asked me to run it by you."

"Okay," Bob's voice crackled down the line. "Now you have me intrigued."

Johnny sat at his kitchen counter and told Bob the unbelievable story that Cafe Olympia didn't even have Wi-Fi. "He said their business model is different from typical coffee shops; they're more like a Success University that happens to sell coffee. They only want to attract people who want to go there to learn about success, not people who are looking for a place to work. Then he said that a business needs to cater to their best customers, the ones who are a great fit for what they offer. Not just try to please every customer."

"It's interesting that you just had that conversation," Bob replied after Johnny finally grew silent. "Why don't I answer your question tomorrow when we're with your team?"

"Sure. Sounds good. Thanks again for your help, Bob."

"See you tomorrow."

The next morning, Bob Hall met Johnny's team and spent a few minutes asking everyone about how they were using his systems and whether they had any questions or concerns. Everyone agreed that Bob's systems were much better than their old ones, but they were concerned about when they would start seeing an increase in production.

"I'm impressed at how quickly and thoroughly you've switched over to my system." He gave Johnny a thumbs up. "That says a lot about your willingness to follow the leader – to follow Johnny, that is."

Johnny smiled and said, "We're following YOUR lead because you have an incredible track record. We're just starting to get a little bit nervous."

"Like I said before," Bob explained patiently, "it can take eight to ten weeks for you to start seeing results. This is a big region – it takes longer to turn a battleship than it does to turn a kayak. Are these new processes freeing up any time for you?"

Everyone smiled and nodded. A few shouted out, "Yes!" "For sure," and, "Oh, yeah!"

Johnny said, "Absolutely. Before, we were scrambling all the time, trying to put out fires. Now, everything's running more smoothly, and we actually have a bit of free time."

"Great. So you *are* seeing results, but the increased productivity hasn't kicked in yet. That leads to the question you asked me last night." Bob paused for a moment before continuing. "Socrates said, 'Know thyself.' The better you know your strengths, your weaknesses, and what motivates you, the better you can live a productive life.

The same principle applies to business: the more you know your business model's strengths, weaknesses, and ultimate goals, the better you can make it productive." A business that tried to be everything to everyone, Bob explained, would never be as productive and strong as one that focused on providing their best products and services for the clients who fit it best.

Johnny was fidgeting, trying to put Bob's words into action. "Okay... So, how do we use that to be more productive?"

"Since you've been able to free up some time, I suggest you make a list of your best and most satisfied clients – the ones who love what you do and how you do it. Your biggest fans. The ones who will happily refer you to other people. Go for quality, not quantity. Be very selective. Only include your Dream Clients on the list."

"Okay, then what?" Johnny probed. He only had 45 minutes to pick Bob's brain before he had to rush off back to his own region.

Bob leaned forward. "After you finish making your list, I want you to imagine how exciting it would be if all of your clients were just like your Dream Clients. Because that's going to be your new goal – to slowly replace the clients who aren't a good fit for you with Dream Clients."

Bob paused for a few seconds. No one said a word, but everyone was thinking about the possibilities. A few of the managers were nodding their heads. A couple were smiling.

"New clients are the lifeblood of our business," Bob explained. "You don't have much time. The fastest and smartest way to get new business is to call your Dream

Clients. They already love you, and they want to be able to continue doing business with you. Be real. Ask them for help. Tell them that you have your back to the wall and you need to find companies just like them. Companies who would benefit from our services."

Bob then said, "Ask them two things: first, if there's anything else you can do to serve them, and second, if they can introduce you to anyone they know who will benefit from your services. Don't waste time with this. Do it right away, and you'll be amazed at what happens. The more you commit to the system, the faster you'll get results."

Johnny and more of his managers began to smile, which quickly started to turn into looks of determination.

"Thanks, Bob," Johnny said. "This is just what we needed. Something we can do right now to start getting results until your systems kick in."

"Call me if you need anything. You all are a strong team. I believe in you."

Bob shook everyone's hand and left. Johnny's team started making their Dream Client list right away, and by the afternoon, they were busy calling their Dream Clients. Just like Bob had said, they were amazed at the results. Right away, they started closing new business and finding new Dream Clients.

Follow the Leader

Johnny couldn't wait to share the new developments with RG. He went straight to Cafe Olympia after work. It was full as usual.

"Hi, Carl. How's it going?"

"Rocking and rolling," Carl smiled. "Busy, busy. What will it be?"

Johnny ordered the usual then headed toward the tables. He was curious how only two waiters were able to take care of all the tables in the café. Bernie and Monica looked to be in their sixties, but you wouldn't have known it by the way they moved. They were obviously very well trained. They didn't waste any motion, and they never looked rushed.

They walked to Carl's bar, picking up empty glasses and plates from the tables they passed. They put the dirty plates in a bin next to the bar, dropped off their tickets, and picked up the orders that were ready. If no orders were ready, they picked up a water jar to refill waters.

On the way back to the bar, they once again bussed tables or dropped off checks at tables that were finished. As soon as any guests stood to leave, whoever was able to get to the table first, picked up the remaining dishes (usually very few because the tables were constantly being cleared), wiped down the table, and were ready for the next guests. No table was ever empty longer than 30 seconds. It was beautiful. Like clockwork.

Johnny smiled and shook his head in admiration.

What made the system work was total teamwork. Bernie and Monica didn't just take care of their own tables; they both took care of all the tables. Consolidating everything they could do on every trip saved time and resulted in better service for the guests and better profits for the café.

"Johnny, order ready!"

Johnny picked up his order, thanked Carl, and walked over to RG's corner.

"Hi, RG, may I join you?"

"Absolutely. It's good to see you. How are things at work?"

"Getting better every day," Johnny confessed. "But before we get to that, would you tell me about your waiters? I was just watching them, and I'm so impressed by the way they work. It's almost like watching a choreographed ballet."

"Sure," RG smiled and led into the story of how he'd met Bernie and Monica. It was over 30 years ago, when they managed a guesthouse and restaurant in Königssee, Germany, about 50 miles away from Vienna. RG's team used to stay at their guesthouse whenever they trained or raced at the Königssee luge track. Their dream had always been to live in the US. Waiters in Europe were extremely well trained; it was usually a lifetime profession.

Johnny leaned forward and slowly nodded.

RG continued, "Right after we bought Cafe Olympia, we drove up to Königssee and made Bernie and Monica an offer they couldn't refuse: we asked them if they would like to work for us. One of our partners owns some condos a few blocks from here. Bernie and Monica live rent-free, and we fly them to Germany once a year so they can visit their family. Plus, they train other waiters for us for when they're gone. It's a wonderful win-win."

Johnny's eyes narrowed. "Free rent and trips to Europe? Hmm, does that make business sense?"

In fact, RG said, it was a great deal for them. "You saw how effective they are. Next time you come, bring a guest and sit at a table. You'll notice that they are like ghosts. They refill your water and clear your table without saying a word. They don't want to intrude on your conversation and ruin your experience." Johnny had to admit that he'd never felt rushed here; when the time was right, he just paid the check and left.

"Our guests love Bernie and Monica," RG continued. "Cafe Olympia is not nearly as busy when they're in Europe." Whenever RG had speaking engagements in Europe, he'd scout out the cafés and restaurants, looking for their next great waiter. A couple of years ago, he found a great waiter in Krakow, Poland – Ziggi Lewandowski. "I think we'll have Ziggi here as well soon," he added.

"You all really are incredible." Johnny looked down at his coffee and smiled.

"So, tell me about your work," RG changed the subject. "Did you talk with Bob Hall?"

Johnny explained how he'd called Bob, who was kind enough to visit their management team that morning. "I wanted to make sure we were following his system properly, and I wanted my managers to have a chance to ask him questions."

"Did you ask Bob about Dream Clients?"

"Yes, and he explained to us exactly what you had said." Johnny's eyes narrowed. "How did you know Bob would agree with you?"

"Based on what you told me about his successful track record, I had a feeling he would agree."

Johnny started smiling. "Not only did he agree, but he showed us how to let our Dream Clients help us find new Dream Clients."

"Sounds like you're a believer now."

Johnny grinned from ear to ear. "We're so excited. This piece of the puzzle gives us a lot of hope. We can increase production through our best clients, and soon, Bob's systems will result in even higher production."

"I'm very happy for you. You're starting to follow the leader, and it's paying off. Following a leader who has already accomplished what you want to do is the fastest and easiest way to reach your goals. It's the shortcut to success."

"Thanks, RG. Now, would you tell me more about your Olympic story?" Johnny was rather enjoying RG's history lessons.

Reading good books and associating with winners helped RG grow and believe in himself. Having been born in Argentina, he'd played soccer all his life. "If you do anything long enough, you develop skills," he added. "I'm pretty good with a soccer ball, but I'm a slowpoke, so my opponents always got to the ball first." He'd played in neighborhood clubs because his high school didn't have a soccer team. Even so, he was mostly on the bench.

While in high school in Houston, he found out that Houston Baptist University (HBU) had an NCAA Division I soccer team. "I started asking myself the questions I'd learned from my Dream Team mentors: Why not me? Why not now? Why not? Why can't I play soccer for HBU? Well, I found out there was a day you could try out for one walk-on player spot. I tried out, made the team, and even got a scholarship! My dad got excited about the scholarship part," he chuckled.

Johnny listened intently with a furrowed brow. His eyes narrowed. "They gave you a scholarship?!"

"Yes. It wasn't a full ride, but it really helped out. A couple of weeks later, during practice, Coach came up to me and told me to go to his office after practice."

RG had done so. Coach had immediately told him he'd had an incredible day a couple of weeks prior when he tried out – because he really wasn't that good. "'You're too slow,' he told me. 'You're holding us back.'" The coach had then said how the new rule was that he would only get to play if they were winning by two goals because RG was a threat to their own team.

Johnny shook his head back and forth and slowly exhaled. "Geez. That's rough."

"Yes. Coach was a real motivator," RG smiled. "But it didn't even hurt. Instantly, my new goal in life became – don't get cut! I realized that I wasn't very valuable on the field, so I knew I'd better become valuable off the field. Overnight, I became the 'Rudy' of the team. Ever see that movie?"

"Sure," Johnny nodded. "About the little guy who wants to play football for Notre Dame. It's one of my favorites," he smiled.

"I always liked marketing," RG continued, "so I started making flyers and posters about our team. I plastered them all over HBU. Slowly, more and more students started attending our games. Some of them even formed an HBU Soccer Booster Club. I always liked photography, so I would shoot pictures during our games from the bench. A lot of them ended up in our yearbook. I was willing to do anything to be part of the team."

Johnny narrowed his eyes and tilted his head. "Did you ever get to play?"

"I played a few minutes," RG nodded, "but only if we were ahead by two goals. As soon as the other team scored, back to the bench I went." He was the first one to practice, and he always gave it his all. He was on the traveling squad for three years. "Maybe Coach thought I helped motivate and inspire the other players by example."

Johnny puffed up his chest. "I never would have done all that. I never would have been a walk-on, either. I should have been recruited."

"That's your choice. Everybody's different. I just wanted to be part of the team." RG excused himself for a moment while he sent a text on his phone. He then stood, walked over to one of the bookcases, and retrieved a book.

"Look, Johnny," he said. "This is one of my old HBU yearbooks." RG turned to the soccer team section and pointed, "I shot all these pictures." RG placed a finger on a picture and smiled. "That's Carlos Quiroz. Carlos was one of our star players. He even played professional indoor soccer for a while. He was born in Peru."

RG's phone buzzed; he picked it up, read a text, smiled, and said to himself, "Great," before continuing his story.

Carlos had been recruited to play at HBU, and he and RG became best friends. RG was a pre-med student then, because his parents wanted him to be a doctor. It was their dream, not his, and it showed in his grades. "I'm saving lives by NOT being a doctor because you don't want me operating on you," RG smiled.

Carlos didn't speak a word of English when he came to HBU. His dream was to be a doctor. "Believe it or not, his dream drove him to learn English and graduate in four years. Today, Carlos is a pediatrician in San Antonio." RG smiled and slowly nodded. "If it's in your heart, you'll move mountains to make it happen. If it's not, you'll be mediocre no matter how hard you work."

A very fit man walked into Cafe Olympia right then. RG caught his eye and motioned for him to come over. He approached RG's table, smiled, and said, "May I join you folks?"

Johnny bounced up from his chair. "Coach Phillips! What are you doing here? It's been so long. You look great!"

They hugged. Coach Phillips squeezed Johnny's arm. It was rock solid and he knew that working out was still a part of Johnny's therapy, a huge part of his life. He smiled, giving Johnny a nod of affirmation. "Looks like you're still working out."

If it's in your heart, you'll move mountains to make it happen. If it's not, you'll be mediocre no matter how hard you work.

Johnny smiled back. "Yeah – almost every week. Work out at the old batting cages. You remember them. Man do I miss baseball!"

"Is that old place still open?" *Dilapidated* was such a harsh word. The batting cages had been broken down back when Coach went to school – that was years ago. He couldn't imagine what they looked like today.

Johnny nodded, "Half the time I go, the pitching machine's not working." That didn't stop him from going though. The crack of the bat, the explosive sound the ball makes as it flattens out around the front of the bat and is sent soaring over the back wall – that's why he went. That's where his soul felt most alive – where the smile on his face somehow travelled into his bloodstream and caused his heart to beat stronger.

"It's a shame the only batting cage facility in town is a dump," the Coach said, "I wish someone who truly loved baseball would buy it and turn it around."

Johnny nodded.

"Sit down, Coach," RG said. "I'm so glad you could join us. I was just telling Johnny about my soccer years at HBU. He said he would never have been a walk-on. On the other hand, I felt blessed to be one."

Johnny fidgeted and looked embarrassed. "Sorry, I didn't mean anything by it – it's just that I thought I was good enough to play anywhere, and I never even got recruited. It bugs me to this day."

Coach Phillips looked up and said, "You were recruited; you just didn't know it."

"What?" Johnny's eyes widened.

"Four coaches from schools with top programs visited me to ask me about you," Coach explained.

Johnny tilted his head and looked at him intently. "What did you tell them?"

"I answered all their questions truthfully. When they asked me about your athletic ability, I told them you were fast, powerful, and agile. When they asked me about your baseball skills, I told them you had no weaknesses. You could hit, field, and throw. When they asked me about your work ethic, I told them you were one of the hardest workers on the team."

Johnny furrowed his brow. "Then why didn't any of them talk to me?"

"The last thing they asked me was whether you were coachable and if you had a good attitude. Like before, I told them the truth: I told them you were definitely not coachable. You only wanted to do things your way because you thought you were better than everyone else. You were arrogant and resisted my coaching and instruction."

Johnny dropped his head and clenched his fists in frustration. He knew he could be egotistical and strong-willed, but had he known that those traits had potentially cost him a great athletic career, he'd have worked on his personality a long time ago. Perhaps it was for the best, he reasoned with himself.

"I was a young high school coach back then and didn't know how to get you to follow my leadership," Coach continued. "Now that I'm older and wiser, like the coaches who visited me, I see that you just needed to grow up. You needed to let go, stop trying to control everything, and just follow the leader. I guess the student wasn't ready yet.

"You had the athleticism, the skills, and the work ethic. But all of that's worthless unless you're coachable. Unless you're willing to follow the leader. When the word got out that you weren't coachable, no one else came asking about you."

Johnny's shoulders slumped. "I don't know what to say…"

Coach Phillips put his hand on Johnny's shoulder. "You just needed to grow up. It doesn't matter how much talent you have; you have to be coachable to improve. No matter how good you are, you have to follow the leader."

Johnny looked down and slowly shook his head. "I've been hearing that a lot lately."

"Everybody goes through three stages as they grow up," said RG. "Dependent, like a child, independent, like a teenager, and finally, interdependent. Some of us stay in the independent stage longer than others. Some never get to the interdependent stage."

"You can go faster on your own," said Coach Phillips "but you can go much further when you're working through teams of people."

Johnny smiled. "I've been seeing that the last few weeks at work."

RG said, "I have a friend who got cut from the U.S. National Volleyball Team for being too independent."

"Donald?" asked Coach Phillips.

"Yes," he nodded. Donald Suxho was born in Albania and came to the U.S. when he was 18 to play volleyball for USC. Then he tried out for and made the U.S. National Team. RG leaned towards Johnny. "Did you hear that, Johnny? He tried out."

Johnny made a mockingly fearful face, held up his hands, and said, "Okay, okay," chuckling.

The team had four years to train for the 2004 Athens Olympics, RG continued. Donald had been cut from the team in his first year because he wasn't a team player; he selfishly wanted to play in every game. After the second year, he was given another chance. He focused on improving himself and on becoming the best teammate he could be both on and off the court.

"Donald came to understand that if he sacrificed some of his playing time to his team, the team would perform better," RG explained. "He learned how to accept criticism, fear, and days when he played badly. His focus every morning was on becoming a better player than the day before. He learned how to focus on things that he could control, such as his position, his playing, his attitude, and his effort, and left the rest to the coach, trusting his team and the system." Donald actually went on to play in Athens and in the London Olympics. "And get this... he was the Captain of the U.S. Volleyball Team both times!"

"Wow! Talk about a comeback story." Johnny slowly shook his head.

"Yes, but the key was that he grew up," said Coach Phillips. "Getting cut was the wake-up call that made him look into himself and helped him realize that he needed to follow his coach's advice and become a selfless team player. He made it his mission to improve every day. Donald transformed himself. He followed the leader, then, as team captain, he became the team leader."

Coach Phillips pointed at Johnny. "And you can too. You can achieve your goals because you have the ability to change. By following the leader, you can get better. Every day in every way, you can get better and better. Stronger and stronger. Wiser and wiser. And before long, you will have transformed yourself into the kind of person others want to follow."

All three were quiet for a few seconds as they thought about what Coach Phillips had just said.

RG looked at Coach Phillips, "Coach, why don't you tell Johnny about Leah."

Coach Phillips smiled, "Have you ever heard Leah Amico's story?"

Johnny shook his head and shrugged his shoulders. "No. Who's she?"

Coach was amazed, "I can't believe you've never heard of her!"

Leah Amico was a great hitter. She'd been recruited as a pitcher for the University of Arizona Softball Team. The first year, she was the backup pitcher and was taught how to play outfield, a position she'd never played before.

Coach Phillips continued, "At the beginning of her second year, her coach told her he didn't want her to pitch anymore. He wanted her to be their starting center fielder."

"I'll bet she didn't like that too much," said Johnny.

"I'm sure she didn't. But instead of getting a bad attitude about it, Leah decided she would do whatever she could to help her team."

Leah asked one of the outfield coaches to work with her every day after regular practice. The coach hit her balls so she could learn how to dive for them and so she could learn how to throw like an outfielder.

"At first she wasn't very good. Leah hurt herself learning how to dive, but she kept at it. Within a year, she was an All-American, and less than two years later, Leah was playing on the US Olympic Team as an outfielder. She went on to win three Olympic Gold Medals."

"Wow!"

RG pointed out, "But don't miss this, Johnny; Leah *only* got to play in the Olympics because she was all about helping her team. She was willing to play wherever her coach needed her."

Coach Phillips added, "Leah says that if she hadn't been moved to the outfield, she never would have made the Olympic Team."

RG pointed at Johnny, "Some of the other outfielders in her college team had a bad attitude. They said things like, 'I should be a shortstop,' or 'I should be at first base,' but Leah's attitude was, 'How can I be the best outfielder ever?'"

Coach Phillips said, "Leah's willingness to do whatever she could to help her team opened the door for her to be an Olympian."

Coach took a sip of his coffee, and the three of them were quiet in thought.

Johnny narrowed his eyes. "Coach, RG said you played pro ball in Europe. Why didn't you ever tell us?"

Being humble, hardworking, and coachable will take you a long way in any field.

"I played for four years. I had to quit because of an injury." He pressed his lips together in a grimace and glanced down at his knee, grabbing it. "Having to quit pro baseball hurt me so much that I didn't want people bringing it up all the time. Maybe if you'd known, you might have listened to me more. Then again, maybe not. I wasn't nearly the athlete that you were, but I was coachable, and I was willing to sacrifice for the team. Because of that, I was able to play pro and travel all over Europe. Being humble, hardworking, and coachable will take you a long way in any field."

"Johnny's getting it, Coach." RG smiled and tapped Johnny on the shoulder. "There's been a big shift in his attitude ever since he started hanging around this place."

"Cafe Olympia will do that to you." Coach Phillips looked down at his coffee, tilted his head, and looked up. "Johnny, I never thought I'd ever ask you this, but since RG says you're a different man now, would you like to talk to my players sometime? Specifically about your story and the power of following the leader?"

Johnny smiled. "I'd be honored, Coach. Can we wait until spring training? I need to focus on my work for the next couple of months."

"Spring training will be ideal. That way, we can start the season with a bang." Coach Phillips stood, shook RG's hand, and gave Johnny a big hug. "I'm proud of you, Johnny. Keep meeting with RG. If you apply his wisdom, you'll go far."

"Thanks, Coach," Johnny grinned. "I'll keep in touch, and I look forward to seeing your team this spring."

Belief Gets You Going

RG and Johnny sat down right as Monica walked over and asked if she could get them anything else.

RG ordered a cappuccino and a glass of seltzer water.

"That sounds good. Same for me, ma'am," said Johnny.

"So, where were we?" said RG.

"You were on the soccer team," Johnny reminded him.

"That's right. I was on the team for three years. Then, when I was 21 years old, I was watching the 1984 Sarajevo Winter Olympics on TV, and I saw this little guy who must have been 5 feet tall and weighed 110 pounds soaking wet. This little guy won the Gold Medal in figure skating, Scott Hamilton."

"I remember him. He used to do a back flip at the end of his skating routines."

"That's him. When I saw Scott Hamilton, everything changed. I said to myself, 'If that little guy can win, I can at least play. I'll be in the next Olympics.'" He pumped his fist. "'It's a done deal. I just have to find a sport.'"

Johnny creased his brow. "That doesn't make any sense. You'd played soccer all your life, and you were a bench warmer – barely."

"All I can tell you is that for the first time in my life, I believed it was possible. If he could win, I could at least compete." RG explained that you needed two types of courage to achieve your goals and dreams – the courage to get started and the courage to endure, to not quit. The courage to get started came from believing something was possible. "If you believe it's possible, it's easy to give it a shot. The courage to endure comes from your desire. If you want something badly enough, nothing will make you quit. I always had a burning desire to be an Olympian, but I didn't believe it was possible. But when I saw Scott Hamilton win the Gold, everything changed. I believed. I finally had hope. Hope sees the invisible. Hope achieves the impossible."

Johnny leaned forward. "So, what did you do?"

"There wasn't any time to waste; I only had four years until the next Olympics. I needed to find a sport." RG had gone to the library and got a big book about the Olympics. First, he looked at the list of summer Olympic sports. Right away, he realized that he'd have to be a super athlete to do any of those sports. Then, he looked at the list of winter sports. "I thought, 'I'm about to put together a plan for the next four years. I need to base my plan on my strengths. My strength's not athleticism – I'm just an okay athlete. My strength's perseverance.'"

"That's right." Johnny pointed at RG. "You were Bulldog!"

"Right. I need to find a sport that's so tough, a sport with so many broken bones, that there will be a lot of quitters. Only I won't quit; I'll make it to the top by outlasting people. I'll ride the attrition rate to the top!" And so, RG had picked the luge, hurdling yourself feet first down an icy chute at 80 to 90 MPH. "I'd never seen the luge on TV. If I had, I probably wouldn't have chosen it. I just had a picture of a guy doing the luge and thought, 'That's the sport for me.' I didn't even know where the luge track was. And surely no one in hot and humid Houston would know either."

Johnny drew closer. "What did you do?"

"I wrote Sports Illustrated a letter. I figured they ought to know. I asked them, 'Where do you go to learn how to luge?' They actually wrote back saying the track was in Lake Placid, NY." RG excused himself again to send another text to someone. *Another surprise appearance?* Johnny mused.

"So," RG continued, "I called Lake Placid and told them I was an athlete here in Houston and wanted to learn how to luge so I could be in the Olympics in four years and if they could help me."

The guy had asked him how old he was. When RG replied, "Twenty-one," the man started laughing. "'Twenty-one?' he said, 'Forget it, man. You're way too old! We start them off when they're eight, nine, ten years old. You should have ten years' experience by now. No way!' I didn't know what to do. The only thing I knew was that hanging up the phone was not an option. That would have been the end of my dream."

RG had just kept talking with him, then, finally, the man said there was a beginners camp coming up in a few weeks. But before RG got to Lake Placid, he needed to know two things: first, if he wanted to do it at his age and only four years, it would be brutal. Nine out of ten people quit the luge.

"When he said that, I started smiling. I thought, 'Wow, this works right into my plan.'"

"What's the second thing?"

"You're going to have to cram ten years of luge training into just two years because the last two years you'll need to race against the best in the world to try to be one of the 50 men who will get to compete in the 1988 Calgary Olympics. Since they'd be rushing me, I was going to get hurt a lot and told to expect to break some bones." RG smiled, remembering the fond memory.

"'I've been cramming for tests all my life, and I'm not a quitter,' I told them. 'I'll see you at your camp.'"

Johnny's eyes widened. "Weren't you worried about breaking bones?"

Actually, as soon as RG had hung up the phone, the reality of what the man had said hit him. RG's eyes widened, "I thought, 'He didn't say I *might* break some bones. He said I *would* break some bones. How would I handle it when I broke a bone? I thought about it for a while, then remembered I'd broken bones before. You wear a cast for six weeks, then when they remove it, your bone is healed, and it's stronger than before. So, a broken bone is just a temporary inconvenience."

RG had reframed it in his mind and came up with a contingency plan. He hoped for the best but prepared for the worst.

"I'm so glad the guy on the phone didn't candy-coat it," RG explained. "I'm so glad he tried to talk me out of it. That gave me the opportunity to put on mental armor for the fight ahead."

Johnny hung on every word, his untouched cappuccino slowly cooling.

"A few days later, Craig, one of my Dream Team mentors, called me and asked me to visit him at his office before I left for Lake Placid. Since we lived on opposite sides of Houston, we always met at a coffee shop in the middle. I figured he must have been busy, so I drove across Houston to his office.

There, Craig had told RG that no matter how bad it was, no matter how bad it got, not to quit. "As long as you don't quit, you've still got a chance."

"I said, 'You made me drive across Houston to tell me that? I know THAT. I'm Bulldog, remember?'"

Craig had laughed and said even bulldogs need to be reminded of that once in a while. He then gave RG his card to take to Lake Placid, telling him that if he was having a bad day at the track to give him a call; he'd get RG back on his sled.

"I took Craig's card, shook his hand, and thanked him, but I was thinking, 'I'm not going to have to call *you.*' Well, when I got to Lake Placid, I called him almost every day!"

Johnny smirked and said, "Sounds like you had trouble following the leader when you were young too."

RG nodded slowly with a pained expression. "I struggled with that for years. My tenacity helped me get through the first few years when I was learning how to luge, but that same tenacity made me very independent. That's a nice way of saying I didn't like people telling me what to do. I liked to be in control.

Even so, before RG went to Lake Placid, he'd promised himself that he would submit to his coach's leadership. After all, who was he to question the Olympic coaches? But it was hard for him to follow their advice. "And I paid the price," RG said grimly. "The first couple of years, I broke my foot twice, my knee, my elbow, my hand, my thumb, and a couple of ribs."

Dmitry walked up smiling and said, "RG was stubborn as a mule back then."

"You two knew each other?!" asked Johnny, amazed.

RG stood and put his arm around Dmitry's shoulders. "Dmitry was my first luge coach. He helped me get to my first Olympics, Calgary 1988."

Johnny's jaw dropped. "You're an Olympic Coach? No wonder you knew so much about the luge sleds!"

"I was the Junior National Team Coach back then, Dmitry explained. "RG showed up to Lake Placid just a couple of months after seeing Scott Hamilton win the Gold

Medal. That was smart of him. He took action while he was excited. Most people question themselves so much that the excitement dies down and they quit before they even get started."

"I was good at seeking out the right mentors," said RG, "but I wasn't very good at following their advice... Part of me always held back. I just couldn't trust, let go, and follow their advice right away."

Dmitry frowned. "If you had just listened right away, you wouldn't have gotten hurt nearly as much." He raised his chin, nodded proudly, and smiled. "But you kept coming back like a champion. You weren't going to let anything keep you from achieving your dream."

"How do you even learn how to luge?" asked Johnny.

"My first luge camp was in the spring. We slid on wheeled sleds from the half-mile point of the old bobsled track. We'd hit speeds of 50 to 55 MPH. All we wore were tennis shoes, shorts, and a t-shirt... and a helmet, but that was for decoration. If you crash on the concrete track at 50 MPH, it's straight to the hospital."

"We call this the 'weeding out process' in the sport of luge," Dmitry smiled.

"A funny thing started happening." RG slowly shook his head back and forth. "Every day, fewer people were showing up for practice. They were actually quitting on their dream." RG couldn't believe it at the time. Perhaps they hadn't wanted it as badly as he had, he reasoned. Maybe they weren't smart enough to call someone when they were struggling.

"I don't know why they quit," RG shrugged. "Some of them quit for the dumbest reasons. When we finished our first run, the Junior U.S. Team got on trucks that drove them back to the top. But us newbies had to hike back up carrying our sleds. A couple of guys quit at that point because they thought they were too good to have to hike back up." He shook his head. "Incredible."

"We make it hard at the beginning because we want to know who has the desire," added Dmitry. "Who's willing to fight for their dream. The faster the wannabes quit, the more time we can spend with the ones willing to pay the price."

"They did that in my high school sports teams too," said Johnny, remembering the brutality of the first couple of weeks of practice each season. The coach worked the players to death because he wanted to find out who his real team would be. "It feels like a military boot camp."

"That's right," said Dmitry. "Coach always wants to know who his real team is. Every coach is impressed by players who have a strong work ethic and who are coachable. Players who follow the leader."

"The beginner lugers all had great reasons for quitting," said RG. "They rationalized it real well: 'It's too hard. It's too cold. It's too expensive. I miss my family. I don't like the luge.'"

"Whenever you rationalize something," said Dmitry, "you're just saying something that sounds good. A rationalization is telling yourself a rational lie."

Back then, RG didn't like the luge either. "I was killing myself out there," he explained. "But I realized that the luge was probably the only vehicle that could get me to the Olympics."

So, there he was, carrying his sled back up the mountain after his first wheeled luge run ever. Since it was springtime, a few tourists were watching them train. As he was walking back up the track after his first run, he came face to face with an older man who had just seen RG slide down the mountain. Their eyes met, and RG told him, serious as a heart attack, "I'm going to be in the Olympics in four years."

"He looked at me, paused, and then said, 'Son, I think you're going to make it. I can see the passion in your eyes.'"

Dmitry asked, "Can people see the passion in your eyes when you tell them about your goals and dreams, Johnny? He pointed at Johnny. "How do you expect others to get excited about your goals and dreams if *you're* not excited about them?"

Johnny nodded, pondering the question but remaining silent in thought.

RG continued, "Four years and a few broken bones later, I was marching into the Opening Ceremonies of the 1988 Calgary Winter Olympics. I felt so happy, so proud, but at the same time, I felt sad for the ones who had quit. After all, what were they feeling now?"

"I'll tell you how they felt," said Dmitry. "The ones who quit along the way were watching the Olympics on TV. I'll bet they felt sick inside. I'll bet it hurt so much that they had to change channels. I'll bet they can't watch the Olympics for the rest of their lives. The regret must be eating them up. I'll bet every time they think about the Olympics, they ask themselves, 'What if I hadn't quit?' On their deathbed, they'll be thinking, 'What if?' Their decision to quit will haunt them forever."

Johnny took notes.

"I paid a huge price to make it to the Olympics." RG paused. "Johnny, everyone will pay a huge price for success. The price of success is non-negotiable, but the price of regret is hundreds of times bigger. If you dedicate your life to pursuing your dream, you'll make your life an adventure."

*"Desire is the starting point
of all achievement, not a hope,
not a wish, but a keen pulsating desire
which transcends everything."*

Napoleon Hill

Desire Keeps You Going

"What would you all say is the key to success?" asked Johnny.

Dmitry curled his lip. "Everyone thinks there's a Silver Bullet that leads to success," he said. "But there are many keys to success. You have to have a dream – not just any dream, but a dream that takes your breath away, a dream that you're willing to fight for. You have to follow a leader who's done what you want to achieve. You have to believe in yourself. You have to take massive action with singleness of purpose. And finally, you have to have the attitude that you are willing to do whatever it takes for as long as it takes. Then and only then is success realistic."

"More than anything else," RG added, "your desire will determine if you will make it. Napoleon Hill said, 'Desire is the starting point of all achievement, not a hope, not a wish, but a keen pulsating desire which transcends everything.'"

RG looked pointedly at Johnny. "How badly do you want it, Johnny? Is your dream something that you'd like to do? Is it something that would be nice to do? Or is it something that you are obsessed about, something that you *must* do?"

Johnny was about to reply but found he had no immediate answer. RG took that as an invitation to continue. "Your desire will determine whether you'll realize your dream because how badly you want something determines what will make you quit. Burning desire allows a person with average ability to successfully compete with those who have far more ability."

He pressed on without pause. "Desire allows you to give it everything you've got. It helps you reach your full potential. Intense desire allows people to win against overwhelming odds." If your dream is not an obsession, RG explained, then as soon as you come across obstacles, you'll quit. Weak desires produce weak results because as soon as the challenge of reaching your dream becomes an inconvenience, you'll give up.

"Trust me," he added, "success is not convenient. In order to succeed, you'll need to inconvenience yourself in a big way – for a long time. That's why it's so important to be driven, excited, and passionate about your dream. If your 'why' is big enough, the 'how' will take care of itself."

Johnny leaned in. "I never realized desire was so important."

"It's hugely important, Johnny," said Dmitry. "Don't ever forget it." He pointed at Johnny. "Pursue *your* dream, not someone else's. And follow the leader."

The three pondered this advice for a few moments. Dmitry watched as RG and Johnny drained their cappuccinos before RG continued his Olympic Success story.

"As soon as I returned to my room after my first day of luge training, I called my businessman-friend. 'Craig. This is nuts!' I said. 'My side hurts. I think I broke my foot. That's it. I'm going back to soccer!'"

Craig had interrupted him, commanding him to get in front of a mirror. "What?" RG had asked.

"I said to get in front of a mirror!"

RG had stretched the phone cord and stood in front of a full-length mirror.

"Now repeat after me," Craig had said. "'No matter how bad it is and how bad it gets, I'm going to make it!'"

"I felt like an idiot staring at myself in the mirror," RG chuckled dryly. "In the most wimpy, wishy-washy way

84

possible, I said, 'No matter how bad it is and how bad it gets, I'm going to make it!'"

"C'mon! Say it like you mean it'" Craig had said to me. 'You're Mr. Olympic Man! That's all you ever talk about! Are you going to do it or not?'"

"I got serious, 'No matter how bad it is and how bad it gets, I'm going to make it!'

'Again! Louder!' So I turned to the mirror and shouted, 'No matter how bad it is and how bad it gets, I'm going to make it!'

"And again and again and again I said it over and over. The first time I said it, I felt like an idiot. After repeating the phrase five times, I thought, 'Hey, I'm feeling kind of good. I'm standing a little bit straighter.' After saying it ten times, I jumped up in the air and shouted, 'I don't care what happens. I'm going to make it. I can break both legs. Bones heal. I'll come back, and I'll make it.'" RG pumped his fist, "'I WILL be an Olympian!'"

RG slammed his fist on the table in enthusiasm. "That's when I became an Olympian in my mind. That's when I burned all the bridges and became totally committed to my dream. Right there and then, I made a decision that from that point on, I was going to treat a broken bone like a temporary inconvenience. A broken bone was not going to make me quit. It was not even going to affect my attitude; it was only going to make me tougher inside. You have to learn to meet hard times with a harder will."

It was amazing what happened to your self-belief when you got eyeball to eyeball with yourself and forcibly told yourself what you would accomplish. "It's amazing. Johnny, you have to try it."

"Only wait until everyone leaves your home before doing it," added Dmitry. "Otherwise, they'll think you're nuts." He winked.

They all laughed.

"The spring camp was only a couple of weeks long," RG continued. "The purpose was for us to learn the basics of how to drive a luge sled. We also did a lot of physical training. We were busy all day long."

"Remember the disorientation training?" asked Dmitry.

"Sure I do," RG nodded. "I loved it because it was so unique."

Johnny tilted his head. "What's disorientation training?"

"When you are high up on a curve, pulling up to 6 Gs, it's very important to be able to know where you are in space," explained Dmitry. "To develop this feel, we do exercises similar to what the Sputnik cosmonauts used to do: lots of spinning, rolls, cartwheels, and even obstacle courses where you have to spin and roll between obstacles to train your brain to be able to operate when you are dizzy. I learned these exercises when I lived in Ukraine."

"Coach was great," RG smiled. "He worked us hard, but he made sure we had fun. He's still a big kid!"

"It's a tough sport. You have to be tough on yourself, but you need to balance it with fun," Dmitry added.

How to Be Your Best

RG drained his coffee cup, smacked his lips, and continued with his story.

When the luge season started in October, he'd gone back to Lake Placid to start learning how to slide on ice. The difference between sliding on wheels and on ice was exactly like the difference between walking and skating: there was no traction on the ice. The sled was so responsive that it was very tough to control. "It feels like you're lying on a bar of soap."

Johnny furrowed his brow. "Do they start you at the top of the track?"

Dmitry and RG looked at each other and burst out laughing. "No, Johnny, that would be murder," chuckled Dmitry. "Most tracks have fifteen or sixteen curves, so we start you on curve 12. You're only going 30 MPH."

"And you crash the first few times until you figure it out," RG added.

"Then we move you up to curve 9, and now you're going 45 MPH."

"45 MPH! I don't have time to think!" said RG, "Crash, crash, crash, figure it out."

"You literally crash your way to the top!" said Dmitry.

"How long does it take to get to the top?" Johnny probed.

"100 runs if you're a good learner," Dmitry shrugged.

Most people quit in the beginning, RG told Johnny. "But think about it: everything's hard in the beginning. So, if you decide you won't quit, before long, you learn the basic skills, and it gets easier."

At first, RG had crashed four out of five times. "Four out of five! That HURT. But I kept at it, and after a while, I was crashing three out of five. Oh, that was a great day! Then one out of ten. By the end of the second year, I was crashing one out of a hundred. I finally figured out how to drive that darned sled."

"It didn't have to be so hard," Dmitry reasoned. "But you made it harder on yourself, RG, because you were half Bulldog and half Mule!" he chuckled.

Johnny's mouth fell open. "So, you flat out didn't do what Coach said to do?"

"I followed Coach's advice eventually," RG nodded, "but I always resisted Coach's advice at first. Part of me held back. So, I learned everything the hard way. When we say follow the leader, we mean to follow the leader's advice right away. To trust, let go, and do what your leader says you need to do right away."

Follow the leader means to trust, let go, and follow their advice right away.

Dmitry shook his head back and forth and pursed his lips. "Believe it or not, RG was a hard-head for three Olympics."

"I got to compete in the Calgary, Albertville, and Salt Lake City Olympics, but it would have been so much easier if I'd followed my coach's advice right away. If I had followed the leader."

"Very few people want to follow the leader anymore," said Dmitry. "That's a problem, because it keeps them from being their best. In the old days, if you wanted to master a craft, you became an apprentice. You found someone who was an expert, and you followed their advice."

"What's the point of having a coach or a mentor if you don't follow their advice?" RG held his hands up. "If you want to be your best, you have to follow the leader."

Johnny nodded, deep in thought. When he was in high school, he hadn't resisted Coach Phillips's advice; he'd flat out ignored it because he was so much more athletic than anyone else on the team that he hadn't thought that Coach's advice applied to him.

Johnny's shoulders slumped, and he looked away. "What a fool. Now I see why nobody wanted me to play for them. And I was too much of a fathead to even try out at other colleges. Geez."

RG reached out to touch Johnny on the shoulder. "Don't beat yourself up, Johnny. You're a different person now. I've seen a big change in your attitude since I met you a few weeks ago."

"That's right," said Dmitry. "Keep looking forward. Ask yourself what you'll do with your new way of thinking. As long as you're green and growing and willing to follow the leader, the sky's the limit."

"Look for someone who's done what you want to do and follow in their footsteps," RG added. "I never would have made it to the Olympics without Coach. You know what he does for me? He takes my eyes off the fear and puts my eyes back on the dream."

Dmitry said, "The Coach's job is to teach, correct, encourage and push people forward. The athlete's job is to work hard and follow the leader. To take action and persevere."

RG's face flushed. "I KNEW that I needed to follow Coach, but I resisted it for three Olympics. I fought it. My need for control controlled me. It kept me from being my best."

"Why is it so hard to let go, RG?" asked Johnny, exasperated. He had thought he was getting somewhere with Bob and RG's wisdom, but all this talk made him feel much further back on his journey than he wanted to be. "Why is it so hard to follow the leader?"

"The need for control comes from fear," RG explained. "Fear of the unknown, fear of failure, and sometimes even fear of success. Being in control feels safe. But being in control keeps you in your comfort zone. You can't improve if you're in your comfort zone."

He paused to sip his water. "Letting go is scary, but letting go gets you out of your comfort zone so that you can improve. When I realized that being in control was hurting me, I was finally able to let go."

"First," said Dmitry, "you realize it in your head, then when you really buy into it, it goes into your heart." He then added, "When the knowledge is in your heart, your life starts changing because you've changed."

"From your head to your heart to your hands, when you start doing it," said Johnny.

RG pointed his finger at Johnny and nodded sharply. "That's it."

"That's it for me," said Dmitry, making a move toward the door. "I need to head home to my family. See you all soon!"

Johnny went home too. He felt grateful for everything he was learning, but he was also a little melancholy that he'd missed his chance to play college baseball. When he was halfway home, Johnny made a sudden U-turn and headed to the batting cages. They were deserted, as usual.

Johnny got out of his sports car, opened the trunk, and grabbed his baseball bat and a bag full of quarters. In the past, he'd always gone straight to the batting cages, fed quarters into the machine, and batted away. This time, he walked around the property and noticed how badly everything was maintained; the paint was peeling from every surface, and overgrown weeds and litter lay about. The old baseball fields behind the batting cages were long gone. Now, knee-high weeds covered them. The lack of care made him sad.

Johnny walked into an adjoining store that sold soft drinks and baseball caps and apparel. The store was poorly lit. Half the lights were burned out, the fountain drink station was dirty, and the few baseball jerseys hanging in the half-empty rusted rods looked old and dated.

The man behind the counter didn't even acknowledge Johnny. A cigarette hung from his lips, and his head was buried in a newspaper. All of a sudden, Johnny wanted to get away from this place. He stomped back to his car, threw his bat and bag of quarters back in the trunk, and drove home.

"Coach Phillips is right," he said to himself sadly, "our town deserves better. It deserves a baseball center that's run by someone who's passionate and proud of the game of baseball."

When he got home, he pulled out his high school yearbook and a box filled with photographs from his baseball days – all the way from T-ball to high school.

He looked at the pictures for a few minutes, then closed his yearbook, lifted his head, and stood up straight. "It was a good run. But this is a new chapter in my life. The best is yet to come."

Consistently and persistently applying success principles will change your life.

Seeing Results

The next morning, Johnny called his managers to the conference room and started teaching them the things he was learning at Cafe Olympia. He shared how his stubbornness had held him back in the past and how things were starting to change for him now that he was beginning to follow the leader.

The managers were amazed that Johnny was opening up this way because he had always had an air of superiority about him before. They liked the new Johnny, and they were more eager to follow his leadership. They were starting to believe that their region was about to become a lot more successful.

After sharing with his team, Johnny called Mary to ask if there was time for him to speak with Pablo for a few minutes. She informed him that he had 15 minutes that afternoon at 3:15.

Johnny arrived at Mary's office at 2:45 – 30 minutes early. Mary looked at her watch and smiled.

Johnny raised his eyebrows and tilted his head. "Can't afford to miss my slot!"

"If you say so," she chuckled.

At 3:15, Mary escorted Johnny into Pablo's office.

"Johnny, it's good to see you. How are you doing?"

Johnny smiled, put his hands together, and looked up in silent prayer, "So much better than the last time I saw you."

"Bob told me that there are big changes happening in your region," Pablo noted.

"The last few weeks have been a whirlwind," Johnny explained. "I've been going to Cafe Olympia, and I met some incredible people who have opened up my eyes to how close-minded and arrogant I was."

Pablo nodded in silence.

"They've been teaching me some simple success principles that have been helping me out at work."

"What kind of principles?"

"First, I met a Ukrainian named Dmitry who said you have to always be green and growing. Always open to learning. Then I met RG. He said that the best way to cross a minefield is to follow someone who's already crossed it."

Pablo nodded in agreement. "Yes, you have to find the right leader to follow."

Johnny leaned forward, "Right! At first, I didn't know what he was talking about. RG said I should ask our top regional manager for advice – Bob Hall. And get this: he said I should do it for Bob Hall's sake!"

"Sure," said Pablo. "To help him go from success to significance."

Johnny did a double-take. "How did you know that?"

Pablo smiled. A long time ago, no one would have thought that he could ever build a company like theirs. But a wise man had taught him the same thing. "I'm so glad that you're open to learning these success principles, Johnny. If you apply them right away, they have the power to transform your life."

"I really want to hear your story, Pablo," Johnny confessed, "but since we only have a few minutes, can I give you a quick update and ask you for a favor?"

"Fire away."

And he told Pablo all about how he'd asked Bob Hall for help, how gracious he'd been in teaching him his systems, which they implemented right away. He also told Pablo that waiting eight to ten weeks felt like a lifetime to Johnny, so he'd asked Bob to visit so that the team could ask him questions.

"Then," Johnny finished, "Bob taught us how to call our best clients – he calls then Dream Clients – to ask them for referrals and see if there's any other way we can serve them."

"How's that been going?" Pablo asked.

"It's been going great because right away, we've been able to start closing new business with other possible Dream Clients. That's taking some of the pressure off of whether changing our systems will make enough of a difference in just one quarter."

"Sounds like things are looking good," Pablo smiled; he was glad Johnny had taken the initiative and managed to turn things around so promptly.

Johnny's eyes were glowing, "We're really excited. This morning I started teaching my managers the things I've been learning at Cafe Olympia. I think that will pay dividends in the future."

Pablo nodded and smiled. "Of course it will. You're doing what good leaders do – you're growing your leaders. Excellent, Johnny. So, what's the favor you need?"

"I promised my guys that if we were able to hit our goal this quarter, I'd see if you could do something special for them. Maybe a party to celebrate."

"You should always celebrate your victories and analyze your defeats." Pablo held his hand up and thought for a moment. "I'll tell you what. I know a couple of the guys at Cafe Olympia. If you hit your goal this quarter, I'll ask them if we can have a private party there for your team."

Johnny's eyes opened wide. "You'd do that?"

"Obviously, you're impressed with Cafe Olympia. We might as well share it with your team."

Johnny smiled.

Pablo fell silent for a moment. "Tell you what. If you hit your goal, I'll see if we can have a special party at Cafe Olympia for your managers, their spouses, and their kids."

Johnny nodded sharply, his confidence growing. "We'll hit the goal!"

Pablo gave Johnny a warm, double-handed handshake, "I'm proud of you, Johnny. You're a different man than you were just a few weeks ago. I believe in you."

"Thanks, Pablo."

Johnny was unable to sit still. He was ecstatic. He couldn't wait to share the good news with his team. He knew it would motivate them to keep fighting for their goal. Pablo was right: these success principles had the power to transform people's lives. As long as they applied them right away.

Johnny called his managers together and told them the great news. He also told them all about Cafe Olympia to whet their appetites. Then everyone went back to work to make sure they would hit their quarterly goal.

What People Remember

After work, Johnny went back to Cafe Olympia. Going there was becoming his new routine.

Johnny walked up to the counter and greeted Carl.

"Say, am I imagining this, or are you starting to become a regular?" Carl smiled and winked.

Johnny's eyes lit up, and he took a deep breath. "Cafe Olympia has grown on me. And I have a feeling that it will soon begin to grow on all of my managers."

"Hey, the more the merrier. So... what will it be? The usual?"

"Almost. Make mine a triple espresso and a quad for RG. Both macchiato please."

"Triple, hey? Okay, will do. You're number 14."

Johnny walked over to the Olympic Torches. He noticed a picture of RG running with one of them. *Wow,* he thought, *I've got to ask RG about that.* Then he made his way to the doubles luge sled in the corner. He lifted it off the floor a couple of inches and marveled at how it was specifically made to race. He realized that just a few weeks ago, he didn't know whether he had what it took to turn his region around. His eyes started watering. Back then, he didn't, but now, thanks to deciding to follow the leader, he knew he had what it takes. Thank God that Pablo told him to come here. By following the leader, he was *becoming* a better leader.

"Johnny, order ready!"

Johnny picked up his order and headed over to RG's corner. He was reading a book about General Jimmy Doolittle.

"RG, may I join you?" Though his visits were becoming custom, Johnny thought it polite to still ask the question before sitting.

"Yes, of course. Thanks for the espresso. You're spoiling me," he smiled.

"My pleasure. What are you reading?"

"Jimmy Doolittle's biography, *I Could Never be so Lucky Again*. One of my favorites." Doolittle was involved in just about every phase of aviation, from barnstormers to WWII jets. He was mostly known for his daring raid on Tokyo. "I've read this book many times over the years."

RG leaned forward and raised a finger. "But you know what? Doolittle was an incredible man of action. Bold action. He wasn't lucky; he made his own luck."

"Sounds fascinating. I'll have to order a copy."

"So, where were we, Johnny?" RG asked, marking his book and placing it on the table.

"You and Dmitry took me all the way to your first Olympics. What happened after that?"

"Dmitry helped me make it to the 1988 Calgary Olympics. Then I started training with an Austrian coach, Günther Lemmerer. Günther helped me get to the 1992 Albertville Winter Olympics."

"How were the Albertville Olympics?"

"Albertville is in the French Alps, a beautiful setting. The food was incredible. Gourmet food every day. Huge tables filled with hundreds of different kinds of cheeses. I had no idea there were so many kinds."

RG took a deep breath, then frowned. "Unfortunately, we didn't feel welcome. If you asked for something as simple as a clean towel or soap for your room, their standard answer was, 'I am sorry for you. We cannot do this.' It was so bad that after our race, a few of us went to

Spain for a week then came back for the Closing Ceremonies.

Johnny's jaw grew slack, and his eyes widened.

"You were that upset?"

RG curled his lip. "Yes, and it made me realize that I'd rather eat a baloney sandwich somewhere I feel welcome than a juicy steak somewhere I'm not."

Johnny thought about it. "I never realized that customer service was so important."

"It's critical," RG leaned forward. "That's why we're willing to go anywhere in the world to find our waiters. Because people may forget what they ate and drank," he put his hand over his heart, "but they'll never forget how you made them feel."

RG looked over at Bernie and Monica, nodded slowly, and smiled.

"What did you do after the Albertville Olympics?" Johnny asked.

"I decided I wanted to do different things. I retired from the luge and didn't slide for six years. Then, five years before the 2002 Salt Lake City Olympics, Coach Günther called me on the phone."

Coach Günther had asked him to return; the Olympics were coming to the U.S.

"I told him to forget it," RG said. "I was done with luge." I'd already done the Olympic thing. But Coach is a winner. He wouldn't take no for an answer. He kept calling."

Salt Lake City would be a great Olympic Games, the coach had told him. The U.S. had the best Olympic Spirit, and RG still had five years to train. "You must come back," he'd begged. "You'll regret it if you don't."

"I told him no thanks, and I hung up. But he planted a seed. He had me thinking about it. Coach called again. 'Okay,' he said, 'RG, here's the deal. I'm putting together a two-week luge training camp in Calgary. You get yourself there, and I'll take care of your room, your board, and all your track fees for two weeks. After two weeks, you tell me if you want to come back, no questions asked.'"

RG smiled and nodded. "At that point, I knew Coach was serious. Heck, in all the years I'd known him, Coach had never even bought me a drink, and here he was, offering to pay for thousands of dollars' worth of training. "So, I countered: 'All right, Coach,' I said. 'Here's the deal. I have a brother who's seen me go to two Olympics, and I've seen the look in his eyes. If your deal goes for him too, I'll go.' After all, we still had five years before the Salt Lake City Olympics. Who knew? Maybe he could make it."

Coach had then asked RG how old his brother was.

"Thirty years old," he'd replied. "Thirty years old?! Are you crazy? Forget it!" Coach had screamed.

"I told him, 'Coach, you've got to see this guy. He's an awesome athlete. He can do it!'"

RG leaned over to Johnny and said, "Marcelo wasn't a great athlete. He was an architect. He was the artsy kind of guy. I don't think he'd ever broken into a voluntary sweat in his life. But Marcelo was mentally tough as nails. That's what made me think he could do it."

Johnny shook his head in disbelief.

"Coach answered, 'Okay. Bring him along.' Then he hung up on me."

Johnny creased his brow and put his hand up, "Wait a minute. Your brother was thirty years old and wasn't even an athlete, and you thought he could compete in the

Olympics? That makes no sense at all. You're pulling my leg, right?"

"I'm not pulling your leg. I just thought that if I could make it, he could make it."

Johnny just looked on, silent.

RG had gone to Marcelo, who had no idea that he was negotiating for him, and told him that, worst case scenario, he'd get a free two-week vacation.

"Yeah," Marcelo had replied. "I could die on this vacation of yours, right?"

"'I guess you could,' I replied, 'but best case scenario: you could become an Olympian. Think about it; you could be The Olympic Architect!'"

Marcelo had thought for a moment, smiled, and said, "That has a nice ring to it, The Olympic Architect."

"And just like that, he was in," said RG. "We went to Calgary. After the first day of sliding, I knew I was back. Meanwhile, Marcelo caught the Olympic Dream. As soon as we got back home, he started working out like a fiend and got himself into terrific shape. Marcelo made the decision to pursue the dream, to take the journey, to face the struggle with no guarantees of success."

Johnny nodded and drew closer.

RG continued. "Marcelo learned the luge and started competing internationally. In order to compete in the Olympics, he had to get good enough to crack into the top fifty in the world."

Three months before the Olympics, they'd been racing in a world cup race in Calgary. RG had just finished his final run and was at the bottom of the track with all the other athletes who had finished the race. They were all standing by a TV monitor, watching the remaining racers. "Marcelo came barreling down the track and, right before entering the finish curve, his sled slammed into the straightaway wall. The impact sent him flying straight up to 'the woods.'" The woods were a small retaining wall that created a lip over the curves. They were there to prevent the lugers from flying off the track. However, when you hit the woods, it was very easy to break a knee.

"Marcelo fell about twenty feet, hit the bottom of the track, bounced back up, smashed into the woods again, and came to a stop at the end of the curve. His crash caused him to decelerate from seventy miles per hour to zero in less than two seconds."

Johnny's jaw dropped. "Was he okay?"

"It was a very rough crash. We're all used to seeing crashes, but when Marcelo crashed, there was a collective gasp from all the athletes. We all figured he'd probably broken both his legs and totaled his sled."

Incredibly, after a couple of minutes, Marcelo had climbed out of the track and limped out on his own. For the rest of the season, he limped when he walked.

"But Marcelo never whined or complained," RG said. "He kept racing despite his injuries. He kept accumulating those World Cup points. He kept his focus on breaking into the top fifty.

"At that point, it looked like I was going to the Olympics, and Marcelo was staying home." Then, on the last race of the season, Marcelo had a great result and ended up ranked forty-ninth in the world. The thirty-six-year-old architect was going to the Olympics.

"Marcelo and I made Olympic history," RG smiled. "We became the first set of brothers to ever compete against each other in the Olympic luge. Dreams do come true if you believe and if you take massive action."

Johnny shook his head and looked down. "That's

unbelievable..." he breathed. "Unreal!"

RG pressed on. "The day after our race, Marcelo and I took some ski lessons. On the way back to the Olympic Village, Marcelo said his knee was really hurting, so he would get it checked out. That evening, he got an MRI and an x-ray done. The doctors found that Marcelo had a broken kneecap."

Johnny raised his hands. "Wait. Marcelo skied with a broken knee?"

"Yes, the doctors couldn't believe that Marcelo could ski with a broken knee either. They said he should have had trouble walking." When Marcelo told the physicians that he'd broken it three months before and had qualified for the Olympics, it had blown them away.

"Vince Lombardi said, 'The good Lord gave you a body that can stand most everything. It's your mind you have to convince.' Don't fall into the trap of using your health as an excuse for not pursuing your dream," RG advised; Johnny scribbled it down in his pad.

"Marcelo took responsibility for himself," RG continued. "He didn't use his circumstances as an excuse; he focused on what he had to do, and by doing so, he not only made his Olympic Dream come true, but he helped create Olympic history."

RG fell silent to let the story sink in, then he leaned forward. "What about you, Johnny? Will you just hope your dreams come true? Or will you make a decision to pursue your dreams? Go for it: it will change your life."

Johnny looked down at his coffee, took a sip, then peered up. "RG, after spending time with you and Dmitry, I feel like I've been playing life too safe. I don't even know what my dream might be, but I have a feeling that I won't sleep well at night until I figure it out."

"You only live once. You might as well dedicate your life to the pursuit of your dream and make your life an adventure."

They both sat quietly for a few moments.

Johnny looked up and saw a big Salt Lake City 2002 banner on the wall. "How were the Salt Lake City Olympics? Are you glad your coach talked you into going?"

"Oh, yes," RG beamed. "Salt Lake City was my favorite out of the four. Their volunteers were incredible. So well trained… and they genuinely cared about us. They would always ask us, 'How's your Olympic experience?' That was such a great question to ask. It was a special way of asking, 'How's everything?' It made them focus on creating an unforgettable Olympic experience."

Johnny nodded.

RG continued. "Sometimes I go to a restaurant and one of their waiters cuts me off as I'm walking to my table. Immediately, I think that they weren't trained properly."

Johnny pursed his lips as he thought about the man running the baseball center; but, he mused, perhaps that was more due to blatant neglect rather than lack of any 'training.'

"Bernie and Monica would never cut off a guest," RG interrupted his thoughts. "No matter how busy they are, the guest always has right of way. It's a small thing, but it makes our guests feel special."

"Coach Phillips used to always say to us, 'Small things make a big difference over time,'" Johnny piped up.

"Small things make a huge difference!" said RG, "In baseball, in the luge, in business, and in life. Small hinges swing big doors. When Bernie and Monica check on their table a few minutes after they've been served, they never say, 'Is everything okay?' We don't want things to be okay; we want them to be great. So they ask, 'How is everything?' That's a much better question. It's open-ended, so you'll always get more than a yes or no answer."

Johnny leaned forward and nodded, fully invested in the conversation.

"Whenever a guest thanks them for something, they don't say, 'You're welcome,' or, 'No problem.' They say, 'My pleasure.' That's a much better answer. It's a reminder to everyone that it's our pleasure and privilege to have the opportunity to serve them.

RG looked out again at Bernie and Monica.

"I'm thinking that what you're saying will probably work in any industry, not just in the restaurant business," Johnny added.

"Absolutely!" said RG, "Johnny, if you consistently apply these success principles, your life will change."

Johnny smiled as he wrote himself a note: *talk to the team about asking our clients how everything is going with our products...*

*"Be more concerned with
your character than your reputation,
your character is what you really are,
while your reputation is merely
what others think you are."*

Coach John Wooden

Guardian Angels

"RG, would you tell me more about the Salt Lake City Olympics?" Johnny asked; he could hardly get enough of the Olympian's life story.

"Like I said, we felt very welcome. It was a wonderful experience. But you know what? I was 39 years old. Most of the athletes were in their twenties. I felt like a father visiting his kids in college. To top it off, everyone asked me if I was a coach! And they didn't believe me when I told them I was an athlete. But I was so happy to be there – until I had one of my worst crashes ever, that is."

Johnny sat up straight. "At the Olympics?!"

They'd had six training runs and four race runs. On RG's first training run, he'd lost focus for an instant. Without any warning, he'd had one of the worst crashes of his career. "I didn't even see it coming," he admitted. "It caught me completely off guard. For the first time in my luge career, I was completely disoriented. I remember seeing the sky twice and hitting the bottom of the track twice. The whole time thinking, 'Please, God, don't let me break any bones. I'm racing in the Olympics in two days.'"

Johnny furrowed his brow. "Did you break any bones?"

"Thank goodness I didn't break anything."

Unfortunately, his sled was a mess. The steel runners had been gouged and scratched so badly that he didn't think he'd be able to fix them in time for the race.

"After my run, when I walked back into the start house holding my sled, all the other athletes looked at it and started mumbling and shaking their heads. Then, something incredible happened: Jonathan Edwards walked right up to me, took a look at my sled, and said, 'Give me thirty minutes and a file, and I'll have your steels looking like

107

new.'"

RG didn't even know Jonathan Edwards at the time. He had competed for the U.S. Team in the 1994 Lillehammer Winter Olympics during the time RG had temporarily "retired" from the luge. Jonathan was coaching the Bermuda Luge Team at the Salt Lake City Olympics.

"Jonathan had nothing to gain from helping me," RG said. "He helped me because he has a big heart, because he's a person of character – a person who's genuinely interested in helping other people out. He's just a terrific guy. Jonathan got me out of a terrible situation. He just showed up out of nowhere."

RG looked up in silent prayer. "Kind of like a guardian angel."

Johnny's chest tightened, and his voice cracked. "RG, I'm starting to feel like Cafe Olympia is filled with guardian angels," he smiled.

"That's very kind of you to say, Johnny," RG grinned back. "You know, it's very unusual to find someone like Jonathan. You want to be around people like that. What if we all strived to be a little bit more like him? We'd make the world a better place."

Johnny nodded and stared down into his coffee cup. He wondered if there was a way he could find a dream that made the world a better place.

Starting a Business

Johnny peered at the bookcases then turned to RG to say, "I just remembered that Dmitry told me that you're an author and a speaker. I've been so intrigued by your Olympic career that I'd completely forgotten. How'd you get into the speaking business?"

RG took a sip of his espresso and launched right into it.

He used to sell copiers in downtown Houston. About a month before the Salt Lake City Olympics, something happened that had changed his life: a fifth-grade kid from his neighborhood came up to him and asked him when he got back from the Olympics if he'd be his show-and-tell project at school.

"I told him, 'Sure, sounds like fun.'"

After the Olympics, RG had gone to his school, assuming that he'd be showing his gear to twenty to thirty students. Instead, the principal walked him into the school's gym. It was filled with over two hundred kids – the whole fifth-grade class was assembled. RG raised his eyebrows and lifted his hands. "Show-and-tell for a classroom of kids had, somehow, turned into an assembly. I'd never taken a speech class in my life. And, here I was, about to speak to over two hundred 11-year-olds for over forty-five minutes – a lot longer than I thought I would have to speak."

Then, something amazing had happened. RG let out a huge breath. "As I told the kids all of my Olympic stories, all the knowledge I had picked up from being a student of success all my life started pouring out of me.

"Half the time, I didn't know what the next thing out of my mouth would be. I just put it on autopilot and poured my heart out to them."

Those kids heard forty-five minutes of inspiring Olympic stories illustrating the principles of success they would need to follow to succeed in life – finding the right leader, following the leader, and pursuing their dream as they eventually became leaders.

"Afterwards," RG pressed on, "the principal pumped his fist in the air and started talking excitedly, 'RG, you have a gift. You're better than the speakers we pay. You need to do this for a living.'

"I thought about it," RG nodded. "Sharing my stories with those kids was a blast. I was being 100% myself. It felt effortless. And the teachers said my story was impacting the kids in a very positive way."

RG set his cup on the table and looked at Johnny, suddenly growing serious.

"Johnny, everyone has a unique ability or area of brilliance; a gift, a talent that's so strong that it makes work seem effortless. But we often fail to recognize our own special talents and abilities because they are so natural to us. That's why it's important to give a lot of weight to the compliments that others share with us because other people can usually see our unique talents better than we can."

Johnny looked down at his own coffee and slowly nodded his head.

RG continued. "Totally by chance, I stumbled onto doing something which used my greatest talent: connecting with other people to inspire and equip them to be their best."

For three days, he'd thought about everything the principal had said to him. He'd said RG had a 'gift.'

"And then, just like that, I quit my job," RG said to a shocked Johnny. "When I quit my job, we lost our health insurance. Quitting my job was a huge risk, but I thought that if I could sell a copier, I could sell myself as a professional speaker." RG pumped his fist. "I *knew* I could make it happen, and I *would* make it happen!"

RG had burned his bridges, and in doing so, he had been forced to commit 100% to making his new enterprise work. "Burning my bridges put me in a position where it was going to be a 'do or die' situation. Burning my bridges instantly created an urgency to get the job done – or else."

Johnny listened attentively.

Since RG's first talk had been at a school, he started calling on other schools in Houston – hundreds of them – to market his inspirational keynote speech, 'Becoming Unstoppable: Olympian Success Secrets.' He had made it a point to speak with the principal, the counselor, and the president of the PTA. "I wanted to create a buzz," he told Johnny. "I called the schools eight hours a day, and I followed up with faxes and emails in the evenings. I was desperate – after all, I had to speak to eat.

"God honors commitment," RG added. After a while, the schools started calling back – elementary schools, middle schools, high schools, colleges.

"Speaking to assemblies ranging from five hundred to a thousand high school students is supposed to be a tough gig," RG smiled. "Being a big kid at heart, I did fine. My theory was that, as long as I had fun and poured my heart out to them, they would have fun too. The teachers were amazed that I could hold their attention from forty-five minutes to an hour."

Business was great. RG was working hard, marketing himself everywhere he went, and he was completely focused – maybe a little too focused. "Being so focused on calling schools caused me to completely forget that the three summer vacation months would be totally dead months for me. I was so focused on schools that the thought of calling on corporations didn't even cross my mind."

Indeed, the three summer months of 2002 had been terrible. No speaking engagements – none. They really had to tighten their belts. "It was macaroni and cheese time. Ramen noodles for dinner time." RG stared into space. "Things got so bad that we found ourselves three months behind on our mortgage. We almost lost our house.

"I decided to gut it out. I figured that if we could make it through the summer, somehow, the business from schools would pick up in the fall. In the meantime, I would start focusing on breaking into the corporate and association markets."

RG's shoulders slumped. He looked down and away. "By August, I was outside the local welfare office about to sign us up for food stamps."

Johnny had a pained look in his eyes. "That must have been awful."

RG gestured with two fingers. "I felt about as tall as an ant. Only a few months earlier, I'd been at the top of the world – competing at the Salt Lake City Olympics. And now I was struggling – humbled by my circumstances."

As he stood outside the welfare office, waiting for them to open up, he heard the unmistakable sound of a small plane flying overhead. "I love flying airplanes." RG's face brightened. "I'm a private pilot. Many years ago, I'd 'temporarily' given up flying to pursue my Olympic dream. Seeing that Cessna flying overhead inspired me. Next time you're down, remember: if you can look up, you can get up."

RG believed that God had put that airplane up there for a reason: to remind him that he was down, but not out. That airplane reminded he that he was bound to succeed big because he was willing to put himself through the struggle. It reminded him that he was bigger than his circumstances and that he just needed to fight.

RG pointed at one of the bookcases. "Just like the people in all those biographies I had read about: Dream – Struggle – Victory. It's the only way."

RG picked up his coffee cup, held it for a moment, then set it back down, realizing it was practically empty. "We struggled through the summer, but we had hope in the future and were willing to do whatever it took to make it. When there is hope in the future, there's power in the present."

"We prayed like it was up to God and worked like it was up to us. And you know, we didn't pray for God to take the struggles away; that would have been the wrong prayer because the struggles were there to make us stronger. We simply prayed for strength and wisdom." Sooner or later, RG advised Johnny, you have to grow up; sooner or later, you have to stop telling God how big your challenges are and start telling your challenges how big God is. "We prayed and we worked because what you do shows what you believe."

Knowing that he couldn't do it alone, RG had surrounded himself with winners and relied on their belief in him to get him through, just like he had done on the road to the Olympics.

"I started meeting some of the most successful speakers in Houston. One of them agreed to be my mentor, and I started learning the speaking business. I found the right leader, and I followed the leader."

Johnny listened intently, no longer writing notes but enthralled in RG's amazing story.

"One thing my mentor would always tell me was, 'RG, done is better than perfect. Perfectionists rarely succeed because they think too much and act too little. Get out there and work your rear end off, and you can always clean up the mess later.'"

RG had followed his mentor's advice. He'd called corporations and associations all day, every day. "Meanwhile, I spoke at just about every Rotary Club and networking club in Houston," he added. "The plan was to get as many people in Houston as possible to hear me speak in order to create a buzz and some momentum in my home market." Little by little, he'd started to get more and more corporate work.

"My business was growing steadily, and then, about a year after that awful summer, the floodgates opened." He exhaled. "All of a sudden, I started getting calls from businesses all over the United States with requests for me to speak for them. Fortune 500 companies started asking me to open and close their events or be their sales kickoff speaker."

Every speaking engagement had led to others. It seemed that there was always someone in the audience who wanted RG to speak for their group.

RG paused for a moment, reminiscing. He'd gotten to speak in 47 states and 13 countries – from Vietnam to Singapore, South Africa, Switzerland, Colombia, and Japan. "Believe it or not," he finally spoke, "only two years after being my young friend's 'show-and-tell' project, I was sharing the stage with Zig Ziglar in huge arenas all over the nation. That's not an 'RG thing,' that's a 'God thing.'" He smiled.

"God honors commitment. There can be miracles if you believe and if you're willing to take massive action. But you have to be willing to go through the struggle if you want to taste the sweet taste of victory."

Johnny leaned farther forward, caught up in RG's story.

"I see people everywhere seeking to live balanced lives. What they don't realize is that the only way to move up to another level, the only way to achieve their dreams, is to get temporarily unbalanced. You have to temporarily give things up to get to the next level. The faster you want to progress, the more unbalanced you need to get. I wanted to get it done quickly, and I was willing to make the necessary sacrifices."

You're worthy of your dream.
You were created to make it happen.
It's your purpose in life. Let yourself have it.

RG pointed his finger at Johnny. "How about you, Johnny? Are you playing it safe? Are you holding back? Or are you going for it? Unless you're willing to go for it, I guarantee you that you'll never succeed big. You have to be willing to fail big to win big."

Johnny was too mesmerized to answer.

"Take risks, Johnny. Take chances. If you don't take risks, you can't grow. And if you don't grow, you can't reach the next level. I'm just an ordinary guy. I just followed some success principles. If I can do it, you can do it. You're worthy of your dream. You were created to make it happen. It's your purpose in life. Let yourself have it.

If you don't dedicate your life to the pursuit of your dream, you'll be cheating yourself – and the world – of your gifts."

Johnny looked down and back up at RG, then slowly nodded.

"There's dignity in being willing to fight," RG advised. "Dignity in being willing to take the journey. Embrace the struggle. Learn to love the struggle because the struggle will make you great and bring you closer to glory."

RG leaned forward and held Johnny's shoulders. "Johnny, I believe you have what it takes. I believe you do. Go ahead. Burn those bridges. Go for the Gold. Make your life an adventure. It's the only way."

Johnny's voice cracked with emotion. "Thanks for sharing your wisdom with me, RG. You've given me a lot to think about."

Discovering Your Dream

Johnny drove to his favorite hiking spot – a hilly area on the city's outskirts. He brought his notebook and some reflection questions RG had given him and hiked to the top of a bluff that overlooked a beautiful valley and a lake.

He thought about something RG had told him: "You can't make your dream come true if you don't even know what it is. If you can't see it, you can't get it. Once you see it, and you dedicate your life to making it a reality, your life will become more meaningful because life changes with the knowledge that you are going somewhere."

Johnny sat on a bench, pulled his notebook and pen out, and looked at the questions.

What are some of my greatest talents?

What do others say I am good at?

What have my unique life experiences prepared me to do?

What do I love to do so much that I would do it for free?

What do I feel called to do?

What would I do if I knew I could not fail? Why?

What would I do with my time if I were wealthy?

Where can I make a difference?

What makes me happy?

How do I want to be remembered? Why?

What legacy do I want to leave behind? Why?

He took a deep breath and started writing. Two hours later, as the sun set over the horizon, Johnny closed his notebook and smiled. He turned his face upward, got on his knees, said a prayer, and felt a tear roll down the side of his face.

Johnny hiked back down to his car and drove home. That night, he had the best night's sleep he'd had in years.

The next day at work, he was as focused as ever, but now he knew that working at Garcia Munos IT Services was not his passion or his dream. Remarkably, he felt a peacefulness that made him feel light on his feet.

A Big Improvement

After work Johnny went to the batting cages. He'd been so focused at work the last few weeks that he needed to let off some steam. Hitting some baseballs was exactly what he needed to relax.

Johnny parked, grabbed his bat and his bag of quarters and went to the fast pitch cage.

Surprisingly, he was not the only person there. There was a couple watching their seven-year-old son try to hit balls. Next to the boy was a pretty young woman wearing a bright blue-collared shirt with the baseball center's logo. She was giving the boy tips and teaching him how to hold the bat. The boy's parents were shooting pictures of their son from outside the cage.

Johnny could tell by the woman's stance and from her form that she was an experienced player. He watched her for a few minutes, then he fed some quarters into the machine and started batting.

A few minutes later, the woman gave the little boy a hug, said goodbye to the parents and walked back into the store. As soon as he finished batting, Johnny jogged over to the parking lot and caught up with the family.

"Hey Champ, that was some good batting. Have you been playing long?"

The boy smiled and his dad said, "Jimmy's just getting started. He got it in his head that he wanted to play baseball so we brought him here. It's a good thing that lady was here because I never played baseball. Basketball was my sport."

"She definitely knew what she was doing," commented Johnny. "It was obvious from how she moved and by the way she was coaching your son."

"Jenny is so sweet," chimed in the mother. "When we

told her that Jimmy was thinking of taking up baseball she lit up and offered to help him out. She locked up the store and started teaching Jimmy all about the game."

The father looked around the building. "We'll certainly come back," he said. "This place is pretty run down, but Jenny makes all the difference in the world. She's absolutely passionate about the game of baseball."

Johnny smiled, "If I'm ever out here when you all come, I'm more than happy to help Jimmy out as well. Baseball is a wonderful sport and it teaches many life lessons."

He bent down and looked at the boy straight in the eyes, "Jimmy, if you want to be a great baseball player, listen to what Coach Jenny says. You found a good baseball coach. You found a good leader. If you follow the leader, you'll go far."

Johnny stood up, "It was nice meeting you. Hope to see you all again soon."

The family walked to their car and Johnny headed to the baseball store. As he got closer, he noticed that the grass outside the store had been mowed. Then he noticed that there was no longer any litter blowing around.

When he walked inside he was amazed. The store looked completely different. The burnt-out light bulbs had been replaced, the baseball shirts, caps and pennants had been rearranged to look better, and the fountain drink station was spotless.

Jenny was busy folding some shirts, "Welcome to The Baseball Diamond. Would you care for something to drink? You must have worked up a sweat hitting those fastballs," she smiled.

Johnny smiled back, "A cold bottle of water would be great, thanks."

He looked around the store. "I was here a few weeks

ago, and your store didn't look anything like this. Where's the man who worked here before?"

"He quit, and I've been managing the store ever since. It definitely needed some TLC." She handed Johnny a bottle of water.

"That's an understatement," Johnny chuckled. "You've transformed it."

"Well, the store's in better shape but unfortunately, the owners have no intention of improving the fields or maintaining the batting machines. Nevertheless, I'm doing whatever I can."

"You're making a big difference. It's too bad about the owners; this town deserves better batting cages."

Jenny slowly nodded her head, "Yes. It's sad."

Johnny hesitated, then quickly added, "I was watching you showing Jimmy how to hit. Where'd you play?"

Jenny had played softball for her college, and now she played in adult leagues. Her dad had played pro baseball for the Dodgers. He'd passed away a year after Jenny had graduated from college.

After talking for a few minutes, they discovered that they had a lot in common.

"Jenny, are you doing anything after work? I'd love to get to know you better."

Jenny looked down and slowly started smiling, "No plans tonight."

After closing the store, they hit a few balls, then spent the evening at Cafe Olympia.

*You don't lose yourself
when you follow the leader.
Rather, you can become better
than you ever were before.*

Focus Determines Experience

The next day after work, Johnny was back at the café.

He ordered the usual two espressos from Carl and walked over to RG's corner.

"Sit down, Johnny," RG greeted. "Good to see you. You look very calm today. Are things going better at work?"

Johnny nodded and flashed a big smile. "Yes, we're finding new Dream Clients almost every day, and Bob's systems are starting to kick in, which is helping us bring in new revenue. The stress at work has definitely gone down."

"That's so good to hear. You definitely don't look stressed anymore," he smiled.

Johnny nodded, then told RG all about how he'd gone for a hike and worked for a couple of hours on the dream questions he'd given him. "They're making me rethink my life," he admitted.

"That's what they're for," RG reasoned. "Everyone needs to reflect on their goals and dreams every few months. When you do, it's like picking up a compass and heading back towards your true North."

Johnny thought about that for a moment.

"RG, what happened after you started your speaking business?"

RG pondered for a moment before speaking. "Well, after about six years, my business was running smoothly, and I got bored. I needed a challenge. I needed something that would make me dig deep inside. So, I decided to start training for the Vancouver Olympics. Only the top 40 men would get to compete in Vancouver, not 50 like before." RG had always been ranked about 45 in the world, and he was by far the oldest competitor. In order to make it, he would have to do something he'd never done before.

"Johnny, remember how I told you that I always resisted my Coach's advice?"

"Yes." He chuckled. "Dmitry said you were half bulldog and half mule."

"Right. My need for control held me back. So, I decided that, from now on, I would follow Coach's advice right away."

Coach Günther had retired by then, but RG and Jonathan Edwards had become good friends, and fortunately, Jonathan agreed to help RG out with coaching on the road to Vancouver.

RG had just finished a training session at the Calgary track. "Coach Jonathan could tell that I looked tense as I was sliding," RG told Johnny. Coach had said to RG, "I can't believe you're still scared. You've been doing the luge for over 25 years. What's going on in your head when you're sliding?"

"I told him that as I see those walls going faster and faster, I get tighter and tighter. I can't believe that I can even steer at the bottom of the track because by then, I'm stiff as a board."

Coach had raised his hand, shaking his head, "You're focusing on the wrong thing," he'd said. "Luge isn't about speed, it's about who has the best *time*. You could get clocked at the fastest speed, but if you crash at the bottom, you lose the race. Stop looking at the walls. They're just scaring you. Pretend you're wearing blinders like a horse. Focus on a spot about 30 feet in front of you and think about what you need to do in every section of every curve to ensure you'll have the best *time*. If you change your focus, the fear will disappear."

"It made sense," RG added. "I needed to stop focusing on my circumstances, and I needed to start focusing on what I needed to do to succeed."

He'd trusted Coach. And for the first time ever, he followed his advice right away. "As soon as I got back to my hotel room after my training session, I did about a hundred mind runs – visualization runs, pretending that I had blinders on like a horse. I only focused on my driving."

The next day, when he took his next run, the fear disappeared. "It didn't reduce in intensity – it disappeared. Changing the focus changed the experience."

Johnny's eyes were wide open. "That's incredible," he breathed.

"I thought so too," RG nodded. "But it goes to show you the power of the human mind. Thank God that I finally followed the leader." He took a sip of his coffee, then placed his cup back on the table before pointing at Johnny. "What about you, Johnny? What are you focusing on at work? Are you focusing on the economy or on how you can be the best that you can be? Are you focusing on how little you can do at work or how you can become the most valuable person at work? Market conditions and other people's attitudes are out of your control. Focus on what's the best thing you could do in the next ten minutes to move your business forward.

"Don't focus on the challenge," he added. "Focus on what you need to do to excel – at work, at home, in your relationships, and in every other area of your life. When you do, you'll immediately transform your experience and begin gaining confidence. You'll start getting the best results in your life."

Johnny's eyes narrowed in thought, and he rested his chin on his hands. "I definitely need to teach this to my managers. It's so powerful. What I really need to do is bring them here to meet you."

RG chuckled. "They can learn these principles just as well from you, Johnny. It's good that you're taking the time to develop your leaders. It will definitely pay off in the future."

Johnny smiled.

"So, you got over your fear of speed. Did that help you make your fourth Olympics?"

"Getting over the fear of speed helped me slide faster and perform more consistently," RG said. "But I was about to have to face another challenge."

One of the Olympic qualification races would take place in Lillehammer, Norway. RG had never been to Lillehammer, so he decided to train there for a couple of weeks about a month before the race.

"When you come out of curve 13 in Lillehammer, even if you have a good line, it looks like you'll smash into the straightaway wall," RG explained. "Whenever I came out of 13, seeing the wall made me tighten up, and I would go into a skid. By the time I got myself out of the skid, I'd lost so much time that the run was not good enough to qualify."

Coach had shown RG on video that he had a good line coming out of 13, but for some reason, he couldn't get himself to relax. It was a mental block. "As soon as I got back home, I called my good friend Don Akers. Don's an expert in how to condition your mind through the words you say to yourself."

Johnny smiled. "You don't waste any time asking for help, do you?"

RG chuckled. "Well, I never had trouble asking for help before, but I had trouble following the advice my coaches gave me. Fortunately, now, I was able to let go and follow the leader right away. That made all the difference in the world."

Johnny pointed his finger up. "That's right. Knowledge is not power. Applied knowledge is power."

"Exactly!"

Don had spent a couple of hours with RG. At one point, he had asked what went through RG's mind when he got to a difficult section of the track. RG always thought to himself, *Here it comes.*

"Here it comes?" Don had said excitedly. "That's it! You're being reactive. By saying, 'Here it comes,' you're mentally putting yourself at the mercy of the track. Saying 'Here it comes' is making you defensive, and you'll never be at your best if you are in a defensive state of mind.'"

Don had said that RG just needed to say to himself, 'Here *I* come!' He said that it would make RG proactive, help him attack the track and feel more in control. "Here I come," he'd said, would shift his thinking from victim mentality to victor mentality.

"It made sense," RG nodded wisely. "I actually wrote 'Here I Come!' on top of my sled where I could see it before all my luge runs. I wrote it everywhere; on my bookmarks, on my bathroom mirror, on my car's steering wheel... And it started working. Slowly but surely, 'Here I Come' helped me feel more relaxed and in control on the sled. The sport of luge started to be fun. I was no longer thinking, 'I hope I make it down'; I started thinking, 'I'm going to nail this run.' And all of this started by simply changing what I said to myself."

RG took a sip of his coffee. "Success is a decision. Sooner or later, you decide you're willing to do whatever it takes to get the job done. I decided to start following my coach's advice right away. I decided to follow the leader.

The faster I followed my coach's advice, the faster I improved. And I was able to do things no one had ever done before."

At the Vancouver Olympics, RG had become the first person to compete in four Winter Olympics in four different decades. Eight years later, at 55, he'd broken his personal best and became the oldest person to ever compete internationally in the sport of luge. Best of all, he'd discovered that you don't lose yourself when you follow the leader. Rather, you can become better than you ever were before.

Johnny shook his head and twisted his mouth in disbelief. "Find the right leader and follow the leader. It sounds so simple."

"Success is simple, Johnny, but it's not easy," RG advised. "You'll constantly be subjected to tests of persistence and courage as you pursue your dream. It's going to take everything you've got. But the good news is you have what it takes. If it truly is your dream and if you persist, the dream will reveal its secrets to you. It will. Find the right leader, follow the leader, then be the leader."

Johnny slowly nodded and smiled; everything was coming together.

Doing Your Homework

"RG," Johnny added, "this morning, Bob Hall and I met here for coffee. I wanted to update him and make sure we're still on track. Afterward, we spent a few minutes looking at all the pictures and displays on the walls. You have some really incredible things here. Mind if I ask you about some of them?"

"I don't mind at all. Fire away."

"What are you all doing in those pictures over there?" There were pictures of athletes and coaches walking down the luge track. In one, the coach was pointing to something, and the athletes were leaning forward, looking attentive.

"Johnny, do you know what due diligence means?"

"It's a legal term, right?"

"Yes. It means the care that a reasonable person exercises to avoid harm to other persons, their property, or to themselves. In other words, doing your homework to avoid harm."

"It sounds a bit like what I've been doing with Bob Hall: learning his systems but bringing him in to make sure we're on the right track."

"Yes. Doing your due diligence helps you manage risk and improve your success rate." People thought that lugers were adrenaline junkies, but they were actually a very analytical group of people. They always did their due diligence; it was an important part of following the leader.

"No matter how long we've been traveling, no matter how tired we are, whether we've just ridden in a van for twelve hours from Innsbruck to Sarajevo or flown ten hours from Europe to Calgary or Vancouver, before we go to the hotel, we walk the track.

"We go to the top of the track, and for two hours, we literally walk down the track, slipping and sliding the whole way, planning exactly what lines we will take during training. Coach knows the best lines. Coach knows the shortcut to success. We follow Coach and take detailed notes on everything he says. We follow the leader."

Johnny listened intently.

Typically, it went something like this: "Okay, guys, this is curve nine. You want to enter early. At this point, you want to be no more than three inches from the left wall. Over here, steer with a force of three (where zero is no steering and ten is all you've got). Down there at the expansion joint, give it a five; over there by that sign, hold it up, then at the end, crank it with all you've got – but remember to counter steer, or else you'll slam into the wall."

Coach might also say, "Take a close look at the shape of the ice at the exit of curve eleven. It's not shaped right. Notice how there's a small bump here. Be ready for the bump. Don't let it catch you off-guard."

Then they'd talk about "escape routes." What would they do if they were too early into curve one? What about if they were too late into curve one? What if they hit the left wall before curve one? What if they hit the right wall? And so on for all 15 or 16 curves of the track. That was contingency planning.

Johnny nodded. "Plan for the worst but hope for the best."

"Exactly. By doing that, we gain confidence because we know we can handle anything the track can throw at us. When we finally get to the hotel, we don't go straight to bed – we memorize the fastest lines and start visualizing our perfect run.

"What if, on the way to the track, I had told Coach that I wasn't feeling well; would he just drop me off at the hotel? You know what would happen? I'd take a hot shower, get a hot meal, snuggle under the warm covers, and drift into a wonderful night's sleep, all the while thinking, 'Those fools. They're freezing their rear ends out there!' And then the next day, I'd kill myself on the track and only have myself to blame.

"Wanting to win is not enough," RG added seriously. "You have to prepare to win. Your preparation determines your effectiveness. Winners do whatever it takes to get to the next level. They take the time to plan ahead and prepare to win so they can accomplish their goals – regardless of the odds.

"Coach Phillips always said, 'Proper preparation prevents poor performance.'"

"That's great advice," said RG.

Johnny smiled.

131

"The human body can take
just about anything.
It's the mind you have to convince."

Vince Lombardi

The Top of Africa

Johnny stood and scanned the café.

"What about those pictures over there, RG?" He pointed to some pictures of a mountaineering expedition. There was an ice ax, some crampons, and some coiled climbing rope mounted next to the pictures.

"After about a 20-year wait on my bucket list, I was finally able to check off climbing the highest mountain in Africa, Mt. Kilimanjaro," RG explained.

Johnny raised his hands up in surprise. "You're a mountain climber too?"

RG smiled. "No, as you'll soon see, I'm more of a mountain guide follower."

"That's funny."

"It's funny, but think about it: if you're willing to find the right leader and then follow the leader, you can do some pretty incredible things."

Johnny looked around at the different displays around him. "I guess you're right."

RG excused himself briefly while he pulled out his phone and texted someone.

I wonder what RG's up to now, Johnny thought. He was starting to figure out RG's ways.

RG put his phone down. "Mt. Kilimanjaro is a mile taller than any mountain in the Colorado Rockies. Only half of the people who try to climb Kilimanjaro actually make it. The trail isn't particularly steep or tortuous, but with every step, you slowly leave behind the oxygen-rich farmlands and rain forests below as you push towards the arctic desert above.

"Climbing Kilimanjaro is a little bit like climbing a three-mile long staircase – grueling."

Like he always did, RG looked for a guide, a mentor, a coach who'd already done what he wanted to do. He looked for the right leader. Their guide for this climb was Dean Cardinale, one of the world's top mountain guides. Dean had actually climbed Mt. Everest a few years prior.

"Dean's game plan had us climbing the Machame Route, a tough route up the mountain but one with spectacular scenery and few other climbers. We took five days to get to the top – 40 miles of trails."

"Forty miles!" Johnny exclaimed.

"Yes, but with a lot of help." They'd had an incredible team of porters. They'd carried all their gear up the mountain, cooked great meals for them, set up and broke down the camps, and kept them going with constant songs of encouragement.

"When you're taking on a big challenge like this one," RG added, "you'd better have a strong support team in place. There's no way we could have made it without our incredible porters."

RG's phone buzzed. He looked at it and smiled before continuing with his story.

The first day, they had climbed through the rainforest to 10,000 feet. The next three days, they traversed the mountain, climbing high in the mornings and descending to 12,000 to sleep. This was done to acclimate to the high altitude. Every day, they felt stronger as their bodies got used to the high altitude.

Johnny listened intently.

"Acclimating is critical because, at the summit, each hard-earned breath contains only half the oxygen you took for granted at sea level, and you get winded just bending over to tie your shoes. Few people would imagine that simply walking could be so difficult.

"'Pole, pole' is a big key to getting to the top. It means 'slowly, slowly' in Swahili. Our porters constantly said those words to us like a mantra so that we would take our time up the mountain. Slowly, slowly gives your body time to acclimate. You need to pace yourself. If you try to rush it, you won't make it. One step at a time. *Pole, pole.*"

Dehydration was always a danger, of course, and above 15,000 feet, breathing became extremely labored. RG had actually mismanaged his water on the summit day and was dehydrated at the top. Consequently, the last few hours had been extremely difficult and exhausting.

"On the last day, we climbed seven hours to high camp, rested a couple of hours, had an early dinner, slept for four hours, and were climbing again at midnight for a seven-hour push to the summit. We summited at daybreak, took a few pictures, and took three hours to get back down to high camp."

They had rested for a couple of hours and then descended another four hours to a lower camp. As fit as he thought he was back then, summit day had been the most exhausting day of RG's life.

"Will and desire are the things that got me through the last day," he smiled. "I just kept thinking about how great it would be to get my picture taken by the big sign at the summit – on the roof of Africa. I focused on the dream, not on the struggle."

RG pointed at Johnny – what he always did before asking him an important question. Johnny's attention perked up. "How about you? Do you have a burning desire to reach your goals? If you want something badly enough, your will and desire will keep you in the game until you succeed.

"Only when you've climbed Kilimanjaro will you

understand why it's regarded as the most underestimated mountain in the world."

The biggest lesson RG learned from this experience was just how much punishment the body could take. The human body could take just about anything. It was the mind you had to convince. "No matter what you're doing, no matter how hard it is and how tired you are, if you can convince yourself to take one more step, you can keep moving forward.

"Take one more step towards your goals and dreams and make your life a fantastic adventure." RG took another sip of his coffee.

"That sounds amazing, RG! I think that I'd like to climb Mt. Kilimanjaro too."

"You can do it. Just follow the leader," RG nodded and smiled.

Engineer to Mountain Guide

Just then, a trim and sunburned man walked into Cafe Olympia. RG saw him and waved him to his corner, standing and giving him a big hug.

"I'm so glad you're in town and that you made the time to visit us. Half the time I text you, you're halfway around the world. Dean Cardinale, I'd like to introduce you to Johnny Valentine."

"Nice to meet you, Johnny," the man greeted.

Johnny stood in awe. "Mr. Cardinale, the Mount Everest climber?"

"Just Dean, please – Mr. Cardinale's what they call my dad. Now, don't go trying to make me feel old!" he smiled.

RG caught Bernie's eye, and he took Dean's order.

"Dean, Johnny's one of my mentees. He runs one of Pablo's regions. I just told Johnny the story about how you helped me get to the top of Africa. Would you mind telling Johnny how you became a mountain guide?"

"I don't mind at all, RG."

Dean then explained that he never would have achieved his dreams if he hadn't followed his heart, taken some big risks, found the right leader, and followed the leader. Dean had grown up in Catskill, NY. His four siblings had all gone to work for the family business, and he had started down the same road. He had studied engineering in college. As soon as he graduated, he had also gone to work for the family business, making a great salary with generous benefits right out of college.

"But I was miserable." Dean frowned. "It took me just a few months to realize that working in New York was not the life for me. Rather than stay miserable, I made the tough decision to leave my job, my family, and my entire life to go out West."

"Wow. That must have been tough. How'd your family take it?" Johnny asked.

"They weren't happy. For a long time, I felt like a black sheep. But I needed to follow my heart."

Dean had been out to the West before for some ski races, so he thought it would be a great place for him. "I wanted a place that offered a sense of adventure," he reminisced. And so he had moved to Salt Lake City. When he got to Utah, he didn't know exactly what he would do. His degree in mechanical design could have gotten him a job, but that wasn't what he wanted to do. He had ended up taking a job at a restaurant at the Snowbird Ski Resort. This got him a free ski pass and some spending money.

"The first year in Utah was very hard for me both financially and emotionally," he admitted. "I was broke. I shared a house so I could make rent. By springtime, I realized that I would soon run out of savings, so I moved into a tent in the woods. I lived there for six months. Every day, I'd go to work, then return to my tent. This was a very hard time for me. I'd hit rock bottom."

Johnny was on the edge of his seat. "That must have been so hard on you."

"It was, but the bottom's a good place to be because you're willing to do just about anything because you have nothing to lose. I decided that being a ski bum was not what I was meant to do."

Dean slapped his hand on the table and sighed. "I decided to push myself to be my best. But I didn't know what I would do – I just knew that I didn't want to work at restaurants or be a ski instructor or a ski racing coach."

"What did you do?" asked Johnny.

"What caught my interest was ski patrol. The Snowbird Ski Resort is in one of the most avalanche-prone canyons in the country. I was fascinated by rescue work and patrolling." He had decided to get his EMT medical certification and landed a trail crew job at Snowbird, moved up into ski patrol, and later became an avalanche forecaster. After over 20 years on ski patrol and after heading the Wasatch Backcountry Rescue organization for over ten years, he started guiding treks and climbs all over the globe.

"I wanted to be the best, so I went to Switzerland and learned mountain climbing and mountain guiding from the best guides in the world. Then I started my own company, World Wide Trekking. I also founded a non-profit that's built an orphanage in Africa. I found the right leader, followed the leader, then became the leader.

"None of this would have been possible if I hadn't forced myself to face my fears, get out of my comfort zone, and pursue my dream. I set high standards for myself and kept pushing. As a guide, I work to push people hard too. As a guide, I find pleasure in other people's achievements."

"You certainly pushed me," said RG. "I've never been so tired like the day we summited Kilimanjaro. I never would have made it without your help. I'm so grateful because now, whenever I'm ready to quit because of fatigue, I remember that day, and it helps me keep going."

"Thanks for sharing that with me, RG," Dean smiled. "It means a lot to me. You just reminded me that by following my dream, I'm making a difference in other people's lives."

Dean's face grew serious. He turned to Johnny and asked, "What about you, Johnny? What's your dream in life? What's in your heart, in your spirit, in your soul? You need to figure that out. Everybody needs to."

Johnny's eyes opened up wide.

"There's a purpose for your life." Dean pointed at Johnny, "Are you going after it? If you're not pursuing your dreams, you're not living – you're just existing.

"Henry David Thoreau said, 'The mass of men lead lives of quiet desperation.' He was talking about the people who are afraid to pursue their dreams."

If you're not pursuing your dreams, you're not living – you're just existing.

"Dean's right," said RG. "Those years when I didn't do anything to pursue my dream were hard. I was stagnant, bored, and miserable. I was stressed, unfulfilled, and angry. I didn't like myself. I was living a life of quiet desperation."

"I had potential but no drive, no purpose, and definitely no courage to face my fears and take action." RG sat up straight. "Once I started taking action, everything changed. All of a sudden, my life had purpose. I had joy in my life because I was working toward something important to me. I went from existing to living. All I had to do was to start taking action."

Dean said, "When you're not doing what you're supposed to be doing in your life, it's just like when you're writing with the wrong hand: you can do it, and after a while, you can get pretty good at it, but it's always awkward. But when you find what you're supposed to do with your life, it's like putting the pen back in the hand where it belongs."

Johnny looked down at his hands, then away to the side.

RG said, "The experiences you've had up to this point in your life have prepared you for your life purpose. You have unique talents, abilities, interests, and values that only you can bring to greatness. There's a destiny that only you can fulfill. But first, you need to find out what you would love to do. What you would be willing to do for free. What you are good at doing. What's extremely important to you. What you were born to do."

Dean nodded his affirmation, then stood and said, "Sorry, gentlemen, but I have to go. Tomorrow, we're taking a group of people for a sixteen-day trek to the Everest Base Camp, and I have to make sure everyone's packed properly. Johnny, don't be a stranger. Maybe we can go on an adventure together someday."

RG winked at Johnny, and Johnny smiled.

* * * * *

When Johnny got home, he called Coach Phillips; he needed to run an idea past him. They agreed to meet the next day.

Johnny hung up the phone, closed his eyes, and smiled.

Celebrate your victories.
Analyze your defeats.

Celebrating Victories

The end of the fourth quarter arrived, and Johnny's region jumped from fifth place to second place, right behind Bob Hall's region. The whole company was happy because now every region was profitable, and everyone was in a stronger position.

The night of the big party came. All the managers and their families were there – even Bob Hall, Linda Shepherd and Coach Phillips were there. Johnny and Jenny had been dating for several weeks so she was there too.

Johnny was ecstatic. He introduced everyone to his Cafe Olympia friends, then showed them around. Johnny, RG, and Dmitry took turns telling stories about the torches, the sleds, the pictures, the quotes on the wall, the book collection, and finally, the story of how they had found Cafe Olympia and brought it to the U.S. The managers and guests were as impressed as Johnny had been just a few weeks before.

RG introduced everyone to Bernie and Monica and told their story.

Carl was busy making coffee for everyone. A special dinner had been catered, and everyone enjoyed visiting and listening to the stories.

A stage had been set up in the corner where the doubles sled sat. There were musical instruments set up on the stage, drums, a guitar, a base, and some horns.

RG stepped up to the stage, saying, "If you all like surprises, you're in for a treat tonight! Everyone, please welcome Pablo Garcia Munos and his Blues Band!"

Everyone cheered. Pablo and his band started playing; they were wonderful. Pablo played guitar and sang. Johnny,

Bob, Linda and the managers were amazed. None of them had known that Pablo was a musician.

They started off with blues and rock oldies, then took requests from the audience. By the end of their set, everyone was dancing all over the café. The band took a break, and everyone surrounded them, wanting to get their picture taken.

After a few minutes, RG walked up to the stage. "How about that? Can you believe Pablo? The only thing I can play is the radio!"

Everyone laughed.

"Pablo, would you come up here, please?"

Pablo joined RG, and they hugged. "Pablo, I know you want to say some words."

Pablo had a big smile on his face. "I feel so grateful," he began. "Three months ago, Linda and I offered Johnny to help him turn his region around. But Johnny was so proud that he wouldn't accept our help. I told him that he had three months to turn things around, or else. Johnny left my office. The rest of the day, I hoped and prayed that he would change his mind. I was so happy when Johnny came back a few hours later, ready to accept my help.

"Johnny, come up here!" yelled Pablo.

Johnny joined Pablo and RG, and Pablo gave him a big hug. Johnny was on the verge of tears.

"What did you think when I told you to come here? What did you think when I said that maybe you'd find the answers here?"

Johnny shook his head back and forth. "I had no idea how I'd find the answers in a coffee shop, but I was so desperate that I came anyways." He lifted his palms up.

"Did you find any answers?"

Johnny beamed. "Boy, did I. First, Dmitry taught me to be green and growing instead of ripe and rotting. Then RG taught me that the best way to cross a minefield is to follow someone who's already crossed it. To find the right leader. So, I asked Bob Hall for help." He gestured to Bob in the audience. Everyone cheered.

"Bob shared his systems with us and taught us how to find Dream Clients. We followed the leader, and the rest is history."

Everyone cheered again. Bob Hall's eyes watered through a beaming smile.

"Did you learn anything else?"

Johnny blinked back tears. "I learned that first, you find the right leader, then you follow the leader, and finally you become the leader."

"Like I said before, I'm grateful that Johnny asked for help, and I'm grateful for RG, Dmitry, Bob Hall, Linda Shepherd and everyone in Johnny's team. I'm the happiest guy on Earth. Thank you from the bottom of my heart." Pablo put his hand over his heart.

Everyone clapped.

Dmitry stepped up on stage and lifted his arms. "Okay, guys, are you all ready for some more surprises?"

Everyone cheered.

Dmitry picked up the doubles sled and set it on the front edge of the stage, where everyone could see it.

He turned to RG and Pablo and said, "Boys, why don't you tell us a story?" he smiled.

RG paused, looked down at the sled with a slight smile, then looked back up and pointed at Pablo. He opened up with the story of how, back in 1986 when he started competing internationally in the luge, he'd met this happy kid from Spain. He was different from anyone he'd ever met before. No matter where he went with his guitar, he filled everyone with joy. His name was Pablo Garcia Munos. "Pablo competed in the luge for Spain."

Johnny's eyes opened wide, his jaw dropped, and everyone started cheering.

"We competed together in singles luge and roomed together during the World Cup circuit for six years – through the Calgary and the Albertville Olympics."

More cheers.

Opportunities

Pablo squatted and ran his hand over the doubles sled, looking up at RG. "Can you believe it was almost forty years ago?"

RG smiled. "Feels like yesterday." He mock-yelled, "Sorry, Pablo!"

"Sorry, RG!" Then they both laughed.

Pablo stood and looked at his employees. "Opportunity is everywhere." He spread his arms wide. "You have to keep your eyes open and focus on finding it. Once you spot an opportunity, if you decide you're willing to do whatever it takes, it's only a matter of time before you get what you want."

In November 1987, he and RG had just arrived at the luge track in St. Moritz, Switzerland. They had been about to begin training and qualifying for the World Cup Race that weekend. The International Luge World Cup Circuit was like a traveling circus; every week, they saw the same group of athletes at a different track.

RG said, "As soon as we got to the St. Moritz track, I noticed something was different: there were only three sleds signed up in the doubles competition. There are usually twenty to thirty doubles sleds at a World Cup race."

Pablo pointed to the sled. "Doubles luge is a wild sport. Two athletes lying on the same sled. They both steer, but only the top man can see. The top man gives body signals to the bottom man to tell him when to steer. It takes years to develop the trust, communication skills, and teamwork required to do well in doubles."

RG said, "I'd never done it – I'm a singles luge racer. But only three sleds! What an opportunity! I ran up to Pablo and told him that this was our chance. We'd never have another like it! We had to find a doubles sled and race. If one of those other three sleds crashed, we'd have a World Cup Medal."

Everyone in the room was hanging on every word.

"I saw the opportunity right away," said Pablo. "We convinced Coach to let us race. We told him the opportunity was too good to pass up. It was worth the risk of injury. It took a while to convince Coach, but finally, he gave in, saying that if we could find a doubles sled in St. Moritz, we could race."

"Finding a doubles sled in St. Moritz was going to be a real challenge," said RG. Even though they had a track, St. Moritz wasn't a big luge town. The Swiss loved bobsled and skeleton, but hardly anyone in St. Moritz did the luge.

"That didn't matter to us," RG pressed on to the captive audience. "We were determined to do whatever it took to make it happen. I spent two days knocking on doors all around the town, asking the locals if they had a doubles sled we could borrow."

They were essentially cold-calling in a foreign country – in a town that didn't like lugers. They spoke German in St. Moritz, but RG didn't. It didn't matter, though – when you wanted something badly enough, the facts didn't count. You just do it. "I knocked on doors, regurgitated a German phrase I had memorized – 'Haben zie ein doppelsitzer rennrodeln schlitten fur die weltcup renn?' (Do you have a doubles luge sled for the World Cup race?) and I hoped they'd nod."

Eventually, RG had found a man with a twenty-year-old, rusted-out sled in his shed. He agreed to let them borrow it, and they spent the next two days getting that antique sled race-ready.

Pablo laughed. "On race day, everyone came out to see RG and I kill ourselves trying to do doubles. We almost did. We were on the verge of crashing the whole way down. Every time we hit a wall, we'd yell apologies to each other: 'Sorry RG!' 'Sorry Pablo!'"

Everyone laughed.

RG said, "We finished the race, placed fourth, and actually received a World Cup Medal. We'd never even seen a fourth-place medal before – they usually only award medals to the top three finishers. We got our pictures in the paper, and best of all, we earned so many World Cup Points for coming in fourth that by the season's end, we had a world ranking of 14th in the doubles!"

Pablo laughed. "We didn't even know what we were doing!"

The crowd chuckled.

The following week, the word that Pablo and RG had taken fourth in the World Cup spread like wildfire in the luge circuit. Some of the athletes who hadn't shown up in St. Moritz heard about what they'd done, but passed off their victory, saying that they had been lucky. "Pablo and I explained to them that luck had nothing to do with it. We'd simply seen an opportunity and made a decision to take advantage of it. We made our own luck."

Pablo got serious, paused for a second, and said, "I guarantee you that if you develop that attitude – the attitude that you will go for it and give it your all, your life will be a lot more fun. People will be amazed at the things you accomplish. Jump, and the net will appear. It really will."

Everyone cheered.

You'll always work harder
for something that
you're passionate about.

Taxi Driver to Businessman

"Boys, why don't you tell everyone how you paid for your luge training?" Dmitry added.

RG willingly obliged. "Back then, Pablo was a taxi driver. I waited tables and had a series of odd jobs. My last job was selling copiers. But that was just the beginning. Pablo, why don't you tell everyone how you went from a taxi driver to a successful business owner?"

Pablo smiled. "I paid for my luge training by driving a taxi. I luged in the winter and drove my taxi the rest of the year. I did this for many years. I enjoyed it because I like meeting new people and I love my city, so I liked driving people around. But after a while, I realized that driving a taxi couldn't be my future. I couldn't make enough money driving a taxi, and it didn't fulfill me as a person. It was just the wrong job for me to do for the rest of my life."

When he'd train, he'd notice that there were a lot of people who couldn't let go of the sport – coaches, trainers, sled mechanics, track workers. Pablo frowned. "Even though many of them were struggling financially, they didn't look ahead. They didn't plan on ways to create a better future.

"The Bible says that everything has a beginning and an end. I realized that I needed to end my sport and focus on developing myself for my future. I needed to end the things that weren't pushing me forward."

In 1990, Pablo decided that the 1992 Albertville Olympics would be his last competition. That would be the end of that chapter of his life.

Pablo looked down, put his hand on his chin for a moment, then continued. "Think about this: you always hear people talking about the big leagues. But you know what? The NFL isn't the big leagues. The NBA isn't the big leagues. Even the Olympics aren't the big leagues. You know what the real big leagues are? It's your life. It doesn't get any bigger than your life. That's why it's so important to figure out your dream. And that's why it's so important to dedicate your life to the pursuit of your dream."

Everyone listened intently to Pablo.

"So, I asked myself, 'What do the most successful people do?' They go to a university. So, that's what I did. I studied technical physics – software testing and programming. I focused, worked hard, and got good grades."

It had been a challenging four-and-a-half-year program. After three years, a billion-dollar multinational tech company had visited his school to recruit students. Pablo had called a friend who was one of the top developers in the world and asked him what he should do.

RG held a finger up. "Don't miss this point, guys, because it is important. Pablo looked for the right leader. Someone who had already done what he wanted to do."

Pablo continued. "That's right. You always have to look for the right coach or mentor, not just *any* coach or mentor." Pablo's friend had said to drop out of school and take the position. He'd left the university and became a software tester. There, he'd met two ladies who were the world's top test specialists. They had written the top books on the subject.

RG held up a finger again. "Pablo surrounded himself with people who had fruit in the trees, people who got results, experts."

"I worked with them for four years, and they taught me everything," Pablo explained. "Every day was like going to software testing school. I recognized the opportunity, so I was the first one there and the last one to leave. I was putting in 12-to-14-hour days, but I was learning how to be the best."

Over time, Pablo was promoted from tester to test manager, test project manager, small projects manager, then large projects manager. Eventually, he became the company's head of development in India. After that, he quit his job to become a consultant. Then, he partnered up with four friends and started his first company. Then he had sold it.

RG had a wide grin. "I remember Pablo calling me to tell me he'd sold his company, and that he didn't have to work for ten years if he didn't want to. I was so proud of him!" RG grabbed Pablo's shoulders and playfully shook him. "Six months later, he called me again and said, 'I'm bored. I'm starting another company.'" RG smiled.

Everyone laughed.

RG continued. "Pablo's on his fifth company now."

They stopped laughing and looked at Pablo in awe.

"A few years ago, someone asked me, 'Pablo, can you teach me to make a lot of money?' 'Sure I can,' I said. 'How do you do it?' he asked.' 'Well, are you willing to work 15 to 16 hours a day Monday through Friday and 8 to 10 hours a day Saturday and Sunday? No? Well, then I can't help you because that's the only way I know to make a lot of money.'"

"You'll always work harder for something that you're passionate about," said RG. "And you'll enjoy every minute of it."

Pablo added, "Knowing when to end a chapter in your life is so important. Most people are afraid to jump. The fear of the unknown and fear of failure keeps most people in jobs where they aren't a good fit.

"Years ago, one of my mentors gave me some great advice. He said, 'When it's time to jump, you have to jump even if you don't know where you'll land. If you don't land in a good place, you just have to jump again! Whatever you do, don't stay in the wrong place."

Johnny leaned forward and nodded.

Why Cafe Olympia

"Ever since we were young, Pablo and I have always been hungry to learn anything that would help us reach our goals," RG said. "We both invested in ourselves, and we always looked for coaches or mentors who could guide us. After we built our businesses, we decided to partner up with Dmitry to create a special place where people could learn how to reach their goals and dreams while enjoying great coffee and great service in a place filled with history and character."

Pablo teared up. "That's why we started Cafe Olympia – to inspire and equip people to create great lives." He paused to compose himself. "We're grateful for you, and if you feel the same way about our little coffee shop, we hope to see you all here again."

Everyone clapped and cheered. Pablo, RG, and Dmitry stepped down from the stage, and the guests surrounded them, peppering them with questions.

"Pablo, you're a musician, an Olympian, and a businessman. Any more surprises?" asked Johnny.

Pablo put his hand on Johnny's shoulder. "Johnny, I'm just an ordinary guy who got to do some extraordinary things because I always looked for the right leader, and I always followed the leader. That's the shortcut to success: find someone who's already done what you want to do, follow the leader, then become the leader."

Johnny smiled and fought to hold back the tears. Jenny squeezed his hand.

Everyone spent the rest of the evening listening to the hosts' great stories. Afterward, no one could remember ever having had such a special time.

*Successful people are always willing
to fight and sacrifice for their dreams.*

A New Beginning

The next day, Johnny called Mary to see if there was a time he could meet with Pablo. He was in luck – there was a 30-minute slot at 10:30.

When the time came, Mary walked Johnny into Pablo's office.

"Johnny, it's good to see you," Pablo beamed. "I had such a great time last night. How about you?"

"I don't think any of us will forget last night. I still can't believe that you competed in the Olympics!"

"Well, that was a long time ago. I like to keep moving forward," Pablo smiled. "Say, congratulations again on what you did last quarter. You are without a doubt a different man."

"Thanks, Pablo. I'm amazed myself."

"Johnny, you simply took the three steps every successful person takes over and over again in order to reach higher levels of achievement. You found the right leader, followed the leader, then became the leader."

Johnny smiled nervously.

"So, how can I serve you?"

Johnny paused, looked down, back up, and said, "Pablo, I've been doing a lot of soul searching, and I realize that working here isn't my dream. Like you said last night, I need to jump."

"Oh…" Pablo slowly put his hand over his mouth, looked down, and dropped his shoulders.

Johnny shook his head. "It's ironic that I didn't discover this until I started learning how to run my region successfully."

"Life's funny like that sometimes… So, do you have any idea what you'd like to do?"

"Actually, I do," Johnny breathed a sigh of relief; for some reason, he thought Pablo would be angry with him – he'd been the one to offer his advice and help first, after all.

"I'd like to do something that uses my passion – baseball – in a way that will help our town and our young athletes. And I'd like to do it in a special way. Just like how you've made Cafe Olympia special and different from other coffee shops. I'd like to create a baseball experience people will never forget. We want to be the Cafe Olympia of baseball."

"Wow." Pablo's eyes started watering. "That's humbling."

Pablo walked over to the bar and drank some water to give himself time to get his emotions back together. "How are you planning to do this?"

"Coach Phillips and I are going to buy the old batting cages and rebuild everything from the ground up. We'll have three baseball fields for leagues, batting cages for practice, coaching, baseball camps, baseball apparel, and supplies. We'll even sell batting cages and pitching machines to schools and individuals. Jenny will manage the shop and help with coaching. We want this to be something that makes our town proud and that leaves a legacy by teaching success principles through baseball."

Pablo took a few steps closer. His attention was piqued. "Have you thought out exactly how you'll make it work?

"Coach Phillips and I have been calling the owners of some of the most successful baseball centers in America to get some tips and best practices. What to do, what not to do, and what potential pitfalls to watch out for. I'll run the business side, and Coach will be the face of the business – he'll run the camps and the coaching. Since he knows all the high school and college coaches in the state, we'll start off by offering our services to them."

Pablo smiled. "That's the best way to do it. You all looked for the right leader, and now you'll be following the leader."

"Yes, and hopefully, one day, we'll *be* the leader."

Pablo tilted his head and got serious. "How are you financing this?"

"If I learned something from you and all my Cafe Olympia mentors, it's that you have to be willing to fight and sacrifice for your dream. I sold my sports car and got a used car and put a second mortgage on my house. Coach is investing all his savings."

"Will that be enough?"

Johnny looked down and squirmed. "We're not there yet, but we'll figure it out..."

"I think what you're planning would be great for our town. Let me think about it for a bit. Maybe I can figure out a way to help you all out. Why don't you meet me at Cafe Olympia tonight at 6:30?"

"Will do. Thanks, Pablo."

* * * * *

Johnny and Jenny walked into Cafe Olympia at 6:25. They looked toward RG's corner. Pablo, Dmitry, RG, and Coach Phillips were sitting together, discussing something. Johnny caught Pablo's eye, and Pablo waved them over to the table.

"Everyone's here." Johnny furrowed his brow. "What's the big occasion?"

"Johnny, Jenny, join us, sit down." said Pablo. "Johnny, we've been talking about what you told me in the office this morning, and we'd like to make you a proposition. But first, I have a question for you."

159

Johnny leaned forward eagerly. "Yes?"

"Do you think any of your managers is a strong enough leader to manage the whole region?"

"I have no doubt that Lauren could run the region – everyone already looks up to her." It was true; she just needed some training and supervision to help her ramp up. Lauren was actually a much better fit than Johnny ever had been, he had to admit to himself. "I think she'll be running your region for a long, long time."

Pablo smiled. "Wonderful. So, what you're saying is that Lauren needs the right leader to follow until she's ready to run the region on her own and be the leader."

"That's right," said Johnny.

"Then here's the proposition: if you agree to train and supervise Lauren to run your region over the next three quarters, full time at first and part time later, we're willing to partner with you and Coach Phillips and back you financially so that you can start your baseball center."

Johnny's eyes opened wide, and his voice cracked with emotion. "You'd do that for us?... I don't know what to say..." He looked over at Coach Phillips. Coach smiled, raised his hands in an inquisitive way, and nodded. Johnny smiled and nodded back to Coach, then answered, "We'd be honored."

Jenny had tears in her eyes. She hugged Johnny.

Dmitry said, "At first, we'll be equal partners."

RG added. "Once you're up and running, we can become silent partners, or you're welcome to buy us out at any time."

Johnny looked up, smiled, then closed his eyes prayerfully. A tear rolled down his cheek. Pablo, RG, Dmitry, and Coach Phillips each gave Johnny a big hug.

They then sat down and spent the rest of the evening carefully planning everything out.

And that's how the "Follow the Leader Baseball Center" came to be…

The End

What About You?

Do you have a big goal or dream
you'd like to achieve?

Would you like to reach a higher level in your life?

Then do what Johnny did: take the shortcut.

Find Your Leader

Follow the Leader

Be the Leader

And make your life an adventure!

Real Characters in Order of Appearance

Pablo Garcia Munos – Two-time Olympian in the luge, IT Entrepreneur, Author and Keynote Speaker, Musician. Stockholm, Sweden.

Dmitry Feld – Marketing and Sponsorships Manager for the U.S. Luge Association. Lake Placid, NY (born in Ukraine).

Ruben Gonzalez (RG) – Four-time Olympian in the luge, Author and Keynote Speaker. Colorado Springs, CO (born in Argentina).

Karen Peña - Wing Walker, National Aerobatic Champion, Keynote Speaker. League City, TX

Carlos Quiroz – Indoor Professional Soccer Player, now Pediatrician. San Antonio, TX (born in Peru).

Matt Phillips – European Professional Baseball Player, now High-Performance Leadership & Executive Coach, Speaker & Author. Denver, CO.

Donald Suxho – Two-time Olympian in Men's Volleyball, Business Advisor and Mentor. Irvine, CA (born in Albania).

Leah Amico - Three-time Olympic Gold Medalist in Softball, Speaker, Author, ESPN College Softball Analyst. Eastvale, CA.

Günther Lemmerer - Two-time Olympian in the luge, four-time World Champion, Business Owner. Liezen, Austria

Marcelo Gonzalez – Olympian in the luge, Residential Architect. Houston, TX (born in Argentina).

Jonathan Edwards – Olympian in the luge, Business Owner. Calgary, Canada (born in Boston)

Don Akers – Golden Gloves Boxing Champ, Petroleum Engineer, Speaker and Executive Coach. Kingwood, TX.

Dean Cardinale – Everest Climber, Founder and Owner of World Wide Trekking and The Human Outreach Project. Sandy, UT.

Pablo Dmitry RG Matt Dean

Acknowledgements

Thank you for your time, encouragement, and help.

Dmitry Feld, Günther Lemmerer, Jonathan Edwards,
Jon Owen, Guntis Rekis, Christian Atance, Adam Cook,
Fred Zimny, Ioan Apostol, George Tucker, Don Akers,
John Segal, Carlos Quiroz, Mark Miller, Tom Duffy,
Walter Corey, Robert Taleanu, Pablo Garcia Munos,
Terrill Williams, Jim Jacobus, Marcelo Gonzalez,
Jim Harshaw Jr., Danny Brassell, Craig Wear
Todd Guest, Joe Heller, John Register,

and many others…

About the Author

A seemingly "ordinary guy," Ruben wasn't a gifted athlete. He didn't take up the sport of luge until he was 21. Against all odds, four years and a few broken bones later, he was competing in the Calgary Winter Olympics. At the age of 47, at the Vancouver Olympics he became the first person to ever compete in four Winter Olympics in four different decades. His story takes people's excuses away.

Ruben's an outstanding storyteller with an incredible story that inspires audiences to think differently, live life with passion, and to push beyond self-imposed limitations and to produce Olympic-caliber results.

Ruben's appeared nationally on ABC, CBS, NBC, CNN, and FOX. He's been featured in Time Magazine, Success Magazine, The New York Times, as well as publications all over the world. Ruben's the author of the critically acclaimed book, *The Courage to Succeed*.

He's spoken for over 100 Fortune 500 companies and his books have sold over 300,000 copies worldwide.

Ruben lives in Colorado. He enjoys the challenge of climbing Colorado's fourteen-thousand-foot peaks, sailing and flying.

Book Ruben for Your Next Event

Ruben travels the world inspiring, equipping, and empowering his audiences to achieve their goals faster. He speaks on leadership, change, goal-setting, sales, safety, and overcoming challenges as you pursue your goals. Ruben uses his personal Olympic stories to illustrate all his points and tailors his presentations to his clients' goals.

To book Ruben to speak at your next meeting, conference or function, call:

832-689-8282
TheLugeMan.com

Watch Ruben's Leadership TED Talk

FollowTheLeaderTEDtalk.com

For Cafe Olympia success quote signs, mugs or coffee, visit:

CafeOlympia.net

Follow The Leader

You don't lose yourself when you follow the leader. Rather, you can become better than you ever were before.

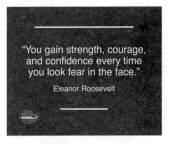

"You gain strength, courage, and confidence every time you look fear in the face."

Eleanor Roosevelt

"A good plan, violently executed now, is better than a perfect plan next week."

Gen. George Patton

Who Do You Know Who'd Benefit from Reading The Shortcut?

From the Foreword
by Jack Canfield,
author of *The Success Principles*™

If I were to write out a list of people who would benefit from *The Shortcut*, here's who I'd include:

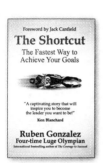

- **Employees and business associates** – for they'll learn how to achieve their goals faster.

- **Friends in management positions** – for they'll learn how to inspire their organizations to excel.

- **Family members** – for they'll discover how to reach their full potential so they can create a better future.

- **High school & college students** – for they'll learn success principles that will help them achieve lifelong success. Insights that are not taught in schools.

- **Athletes** – for they'll learn how to improve their game faster than they ever have before.

- Finally, anyone who has a goal or dream they are hungry to achieve.

For information on bulk orders, call:

832-689-8282

Wheel training in Lake Placid in 1984.

Dmitry cooling RG's steels before a race in 1986.

RG and Coach Günther Lemmerer

Bernie, Monica and RG in Königssee, Germany.

RG, Herschel Walker and Pablo at Albertville Olympics.

RG and Marcelo at the Salt Lake City Olympics.

Jonathan Edwards working on RG's sled.

Teaching kids how to they can live their dreams.

RG (left) after competing when he was 55.

RG and Scott Hamilton finally meet in 2022.